A PRACTICAL GUIDE for Witches

A PRACTICAL GUIDE
for
Witches

Spells, Rituals, and Magic for an Enchanted Life

Ylva Mara Radziszewski

Illustrations by Tara O'Brien

ROCKRIDGE
PRESS

For general information on our other products and services or to obtain technical support, please contact our Customer Care Department within the United States at (866) 744-2665, or outside the United States at (510) 253-0500.

Rockridge Press publishes its books in a variety of electronic and print formats. Some content that appears in print may not be available in electronic books, and vice versa.

Interior and Cover Designer: Stephanie Mautone
Art Producer: Samantha Ulban
Editor: Emily Angell
Production Editor: Matthew Burnett

Illustrations © 2020 Tara O'Brien. Colleen Borst/Modern Hexology, p.18.
Author photograph courtesy of © Megan Xeal.

ISBN: Print 978-1-64739-402-8 | eBook 978-1-64739-403-5
R0

To The Witches Temple, my students, clients, and sibling witches. May this grimoire inspire you to share your magic with the world.

Contents

Introduction

This book marks a very special beginning for me. It's the first time I've brought together my 25 years of experience in the world of magic, spell crafting, herbalism, witchcraft, and discovery to share my learnings with others. This is the book I wish I had had when I was a young witch just starting on my magical path. I offer this book to you with excitement and humility. My hope is that you glean tools and inspiration that can help you further your own magical practice.

So who am I to teach you all of this? To start, I am a temple tender, a traditional witch, a multimedia artist, a writer, a clinical herbalist, and a licensed acupuncturist. I am also a chronically ill, gender non-binary trans femme, a survivor of sexual assault, and an activist. All of this is relevant because our lived experiences are our most important teachers on the witch's path. Even if you are new to magic, you have many life experiences you can draw on as you begin to tune into magic and weave rituals and spells. I am also the founder of the School of Traditional Magic and serve as High Priestess of The Witches Temple, formerly The Cunning Crow Apothecary, located in Seattle, Washington, on unceded Duwamish (Dkhw'Duw'Absh) and Coast Salish territory. The Witches Temple is a collective of trans, queer, black, POC, disabled, and chronically ill practitioners offering free and sliding-scale services to the wider community. I'm a firm believer that community is another integral part of witchcraft—the tradition of magic is rooted in resource and knowledge sharing and carrying on cultural practices of our lineage.

The deepest purpose of my work—and this book—is to help people who are called to magic reclaim the witch within. In these pages, you'll find practical spells, rituals, and advice to help you access and explore magic throughout your daily life. We start with a brief introduction to the history of witchcraft, different types of witches, and various magical and traditional folk practices. From there you will learn about foundational knowledge for the practical witch—from the elements to divination, moon cycles, and more—as well as all the tools and materials you need to get started. Then I'll provide you with spells, tips, rituals, and practices to apply to the different areas of your life, including:

- **Health and Happiness**, where we focus on personal wellness with energy-clearing and empowerment techniques, wellness rituals, and simple self-care practices.

- **Friends, Family, and Community**, in which we explore how to approach magic in a way that supports your relationships, including rituals for forgiveness, avoiding gossip, and mending a friendship.

- **House and Home,** where you'll learn how to energetically cleanse, protect, and bless your temple and most important space, your home, including spells to honor your household spirits, bless your houseplants, and make your bedroom your sanctuary.

- **Career, Success, and Prosperity**, where we discuss the magic of mutual care, resource sharing, and how to redefine abundance. You'll find a spell to bless your hustle and to get paid, plus various abundance charms.

- **The Bustle of Daily Life**, where we conclude with practical rituals that combine principles from earlier chapters to address common daily challenges and circumstances.

No matter where you are on the witch's path—just starting out or deep into your journey—there is always an opportunity to learn and grow. We each have our own unique way of connecting to magic. Allow this book to inspire you, offer you new ideas, empower you to grow your practice, and strengthen your roots. No one can tell you what your magic means to you . . . or even how to be a witch. My role is to be your mentor and guide so you find your own path—and enjoy some creative spells, nourishing rituals, and exciting practices along the way.

1

AN INTRODUCTION TO WITCHES AND WITCHCRAFT

I see you, Witch, harnessing your magic and seeking to deepen your craft. Now what does that even mean? While I don't know what it means to you personally or what happens next on your journey, I have some ideas that will help ground and focus you as you explore your own path as a witch. In this chapter, you'll find a brief history of witches, an introduction to a few different types of magical practices, common myths and misconceptions about magic and witchcraft, and a foundation for magical cosmology, a system of beliefs that can help you make sense of your life experiences and take action on your values.

A Brief History of Witches

When you think of the history of witches, images of frenzied rituals, the Salem Witch Trials, or the 700-year inquisition might come to mind. Yet the history of the craft is actually much older than these examples and draws from cultures far beyond Western settler colonialism, occultism, and the Eurocentric origins that tend to dominate the narrative of contemporary witchery. As you embark on your journey, it's important to understand the inclusive history of the craft on a global level.

Every culture has its own history of magic, traditional medicine, and healing. In telling the story of the witch, there isn't one single narrative. The story comes from our ancestral witches—the storytellers, herbalists, healers, teachers, and wise leaders who shaped our varied cultural practices. Their magic is etched into our bones, carrying generations of ancestral wisdom. In my lineage, they are:

- The Vještica of Croatia.

- The Szeptucha of Poland.

- The Drabarni within Roma communities.

I highly encourage you to research the history of witches and traditional magic of your own cultures. The witch is healer, artist, herbalist, community organizer, parent, laborer.

YOU are Witch, just as you are.

Common Misconceptions and Myths

There are so many assumptions, misconceptions, and myths about witches today. Here are a few common ones and what to know about them.

Good Magic is White, and Bad Magic is Black *Magic does not exist on the domain of binary gender, sex, or moral dualism. There is no such thing as "good magic" or "bad magic." In fact, the notion of "good magic" as white magic and "bad magic" as black magic perpetuates divisive bias and is rooted in racism. Traditionally, Christianity of the West was declared "good" by its followers, whereas the spiritual practices of indigenous, black, and brown people were considered "evil." Magic is magic—plain and simple.*

Magic is Binary *The assumption that to be a witch you must embody the divine feminine or divine masculine is very far from the truth. Limiting or oppressive binaries are by no means necessary to practice magic. Anyone can be a witch, not just cisgender women.*

I have to be born a Witch to practice Magic *I believe we are all born with magic flowing through us. Therefore, we are all born witches and can connect to the witch within at any moment. No one path is the correct path. You aren't more of a witch if you were raised in the craft or were apprenticed to a teacher for 20 years or are just starting out with this book.*

Witchcraft is the Tool of the Devil *To control the narrative of the witch as wicked, the Catholic Church created the Devil and superimposed his character onto old pagan gods. This was to show that those who followed the gods and spirits of nature actually followed the Devil. This is a very narrow and outdated viewpoint. As you'll see in this book, witchcraft is primarily used for good and in support of the well-being of your community.*

Witchcraft is European *While it's true that the word "witch" has etymological roots in Old/Middle English, the practices of witches are global and culturally diverse. Thankfully there are growing resources in print and online that speak to this more accurate history and help reestablish pre-Christian cultural and spiritual narratives.*

Witchcraft and Religion

It is said that witchcraft is the "oldest religion," but in truth witchcraft isn't a religion at all. The craft of the witch is a way of life, and the skills required to practice magic are honed over one's lifetime. The witch's path is informed by our lived experiences and the legacy of those who have walked before us.

Because of this, the practice of witchcraft is very personal. There is no doctrine; no one can tell you how to embody it or define its impact on you. The amazing thing about magic is that it cannot be owned by any one person or tradition.

Much of what we see in popular culture would have us believe that magic and witchcraft are either Wiccan or presented in relationship to Christianity. There are magical practices within many religions, and many witches are people of complex faith.

You do not need to identify with any religion to be a witch, and practicing witchcraft does not exclude you from maintaining faith in other religious systems. Magic is a faithless devotion with many names. It flows through all traditions, religions, and people. Magic has no natural affinity except to that which lives in the heart of the witch. Our work is to initiate ourselves to the truth of our hearts and be honest about what we discover in its depths.

Types of Witches

There are so many ways to be a witch. Every culture across the globe has a name for those who practice earth-honoring and healing traditions. Following are some broad categories of different types of practices within witchcraft. This list is by no means exhaustive, nor are you limited to incorporate just one type of practice within your craft. As you read through these categories, notice your response to the descriptions. Make note of which practices get your attention. Where and how do you notice your responses in your body? What is it about those practices that interests you? This will help guide you on your personal exploration in naming your own path.

Here's how I would identify my path: I am an animistic pantheist who practices traditional magic and folk craft with an affinity for hedge craft and a natural talent for cottage witchery. Now it's your turn.

TRADITIONAL OR FOLK WITCH

The Traditional or Folk Witch seeks to hone their craft through the known practices of their ancestral cultures. These witches focus on practical magic for use in everyday life. Folk Witches pull magic from a well of ancestral and cultural practices outside the constraints of cultural assimilation. The spells and rituals of a folk witch involve charms (spoken spells or magical phrases), amulets (small objects enchanted to ward against certain influences), talismans (small objects enchanted to attract or generate a certain influencing power), laying of hands or magical "doctoring," cleansing and protection spells for the body or home, and the making of healing oils and magical washes for everyday use. Given the focus on community witchery and divestment from systemic oppression, the practices of Folk Witches are also rooted in magical activism.

Hedge or Green Witch

The Hedge Witch or Green Witch focuses on the study of and alignment with the natural world. They channel their magic through working with plants, animals, minerals, and other elemental manifestations like dew, storms, or the ash from fire. Their altar is the wild spaces, and their spells follow and draw strength from the cycles of nature. Their ritual tools are often found objects or hand-crafted from natural materials. There is an emphasis on herbalism, meditation, dream working, trance induction, and communion with the spirits of nature. Please remember that although you do not need to be an herbalist to work with botanicals, it is vital to do your research and consult a professional clinical herbalist before administering plants internally or externally.

Eclectic Witch

The Eclectic Witch doesn't follow a particular tradition, path, or practice of witchcraft. Instead, they sort through and assimilate the methods, tools, techniques, and practices of many traditions and cultures to fit their needs. The benefit of eclecticism is that you can tailor your craft to suit your personal worldview. The challenge of this particular path is that it lacks specific cultural context and can be difficult to define. If you are drawn to this path, be mindful about the privileges that afford you to pull from the cultural practices you are seeking. (I discuss cultural appropriation in more depth at the end of chapter 3.)

Gardnerian Wiccan

Wicca is essentially a form of binary paganism, where the source is seen as the Goddess and the God. It draws on multiple folk customs from different cultures throughout Europe and relies heavily on alchemy, occultism (particularly ceremonial magic), and Western esotericism. Gardnerian Wicca was founded by Gerald Gardner and emphasizes the supreme power of the Goddess over that of the God and a calendar consisting of eight seasonal holidays based on the equinoxes, solstices, and cross quarter days. It's important to note that Wicca in particular is rife with controversy from historic allegations of misconduct and misappropriation of cultural practices. Because of this, it's very important seekers be discerning of their communities and resources if they are drawn to this path. Always take care to protect yourself.

ALEXANDRIAN WICCAN

This form of Wicca was founded by Alexander and Maxine Sanders and focuses on equality between the God and Goddess. It draws more heavily on ceremonial magic.

KITCHEN WITCH

The path of the Kitchen Witch is a little bit Hedge Witch, a little bit Green Witchery, and a whole lot of folk magic for flavor. The altar of the Kitchen Witch is their home. The Kitchen Witch will bless all of their herbs before cooking a meal for community or serving up tea for guests. This witch always has food for company and the perfect herbal tea blend for any situation or conversation. Their magic is the spark of the hearth, and they bring it everywhere they go. They can make the most mundane tasks magical, harnessing joy in the comforts of everyday tasks. Their home is a temple for anyone who needs sanctuary, and somehow whenever they visit your home, it instantly feels brighter and safer. Although solitary in practice, the Kitchen Witch often finds themselves in a warm home surrounded by caring folx.

CEREMONIAL WITCH

The Ceremonial Witch draws upon complex systems of mysticism and esoterica to seek deeper states of wisdom. They apply this wisdom to elaborate ceremonies and complex rituals that often involve communion with archetypes and unlocking arcane mysteries within their own mind. Ceremonial Witchcraft can be more intellectual, drawing from occultism, complex sigils, medieval esoteric thought, and alchemy as well as Egyptian and Quabbalistic magic in crafting their rituals. The spells of Ceremonial Witchcraft can be very liturgical and complex.

HEREDITARY WITCH

A Hereditary Witch is one who is brought up in the craft and taught the ways of the witch by a family member or caregiver. Hereditary Witches often come from a long and unbroken line of magical tradition. Their spells and rituals have been passed down from generation to generation; their practice is unique to their family. Hereditary Witches have a strong cultural connection to their traditional ancestral practices and folk customs. It's important to distinguish between hereditary witches and hereditary magic. For example, my grandmother would never say that she was a witch. However, I grew up with her practicing aspects of Kitchen Witchery, employing charms, rituals, and superstitions in her cooking, housekeeping, and caring of her grandchildren. She learned these things from her parents, who likely learned them from their parents. The hidden treasures of Hereditary Witchery can be subtle until you look for them.

Finding Your Way to the Craft

Remember: No one can tell you that you are a witch. You either are or you are not, and it's completely up to you. Study and ask questions. Reflect on the answers you find. Spend time with a practice before you dedicate yourself to it or its community. Take your time exploring. Feel what resonates deeply. If you find that something is not for you, return it with gratitude and move on. Do this with respect and remember that your own path as a witch will always be evolving.

The Sharing of Knowledge and Rituals

Magic lives inside of us; its practice is a continual ritual of remembering this. A witch is someone who is born knowing to ask questions, seek answers, and honor the wisdom of nature. So much of witchcraft involves listening to your own intuition. In fact, in Balkan witchcraft it is said that most witches gain power through self-initiation. But how do we learn other aspects of the practice? Learning magic can feel complicated. For me, I learned a lot about the craft from trial and error supplemented by the writings and teachings of sibling witches. If there's something specific you want to learn, seek guidance from someone who has traveled that path.

I was blessed to have found a teacher, Jackie McCloskey, at a young age, to whom I was apprenticed for 19 years before she died. Finding the "right" community is a journey and vital to your experience. Many witches seek out covens (a formally established and intimate group of witches) to learn the craft. You can also follow online communities such as The HoodWitch, Patheos, and WitchVox to meet other witches and learn more about magic or attend conferences like the Modern Witches Confluence and the Salem Witchcraft and Folklore Festival. There are some wonderful schools and podcasts out there as well. For some of my favorite witchy sources, check out the Resources section at the back of this book.

Finding the Magic in Everyday Life

Our modern world is troubled. Sadly, we find ourselves in the grip of unprecedented global strife and crisis. At times it can feel overwhelming or impossible to access joy or hope. Yet the work of the witch is to draw strength from the past and the natural world and cast that blessing into our current reality as a seed of hope. We must remember, as

Dr. Clarissa Pinokla Estes writes in her essay of the same title, *we were made for these times.* There may not have ever been a more vital time to access magic. The world needs you, Witch.

The following chapters will help you bring practical magic to your daily tasks and interactions through simple spells and rituals. The book is easy to follow in order to help you start bettering your life—and the world—right away.

Whether blessing your shampoo and soaps so each shower is an energetic cleansing, bundling protective herbs above your entryway for safety, or anointing your cards and cash with abundance oils to encourage your success, our modern craft is a way to enchant your everyday life.

2

ESSENTIAL KNOWLEDGE FOR THE PRACTICAL WITCH

In this chapter, you'll learn about the most important practical foundations of witchcraft. This includes everything from spells, manifestations, setting intentions, and altars to the seasons, moon phases, elements, colors, divinations, and more.

Take time to explore why and how certain spells, rituals, or practices work for you before adopting them into your practice. If something doesn't work for you, that's also great to know. Finally, consider what might work better—this is where your creativity comes into play. As you already learned in chapter 1, there is no right or wrong way to be a witch.

As with any craft, as the crafter grows more skilled, they are able to alter and tailor techniques to best suit their creative vision and preferred ways of working. The same holds true for witchcraft. Once you have command of the essential elements, put your personal spin on the craft and cater to your unique skills and passions.

The Lowdown on Spells

Now we're getting to the fun stuff. Everyone wants to know about spells! First and foremost, remember that the stronger your relationship is to the ingredients, methods, and intentions of a spell, the stronger and deeper the impact of your spell will be. Here are some key principles to remember when it comes to spellcasting and customizing or crafting your own spells.

* **Focus.** "Energy follows intent" is a popular adage in New Age doctrine. I actually believe that energy follows attention. The more attention you give your ingredients and process, the deeper the impact of the spell will be.

* **Ingredients.** The best ingredients for a spell are those that you are in relationship with. If you don't know how to work with an ingredient, spend time studying its properties. Choose ingredients that embody the purpose of the intention of your spell. Every component of a spell contributes to its overall effect. Each ingredient must be blessed, honored, and charged to align with the intent of the ritual.

★ Magical Correspondences ★

You'll see the term "correspondence" used a lot throughout this book. A correspondence refers to a shared resonance between objects or ingredients. For example, mugwort is often worked with to harness the energy of the moon, the planet Venus, and the wisdom of elderhood. Those would be the correspondences of mugwort. Or we work with particular elements or colors because of their relevant correspondences—such as white for healing or blue for protection.

- **Timing.** The craft will find purpose and direction according to the unique will of each witch. Yet there are still universal forces at play that will affect your practice regardless of your intentions. Tracking these forces—which include the season, time of day, moon phase, and more—will help you determine the most appropriate timing for your workings.

- **Impact.** Every spell has an intended outcome. Everything we do or say has consequences—and this is particularly true for spellcasting. So take your spells seriously. Your personal value system determines the morality of your choices. Remember that every action has impact. Track yours responsibly and be accountable for your choices.

- **Attachment.** Magic is full of paradox. While we need to bring our full focus to our spells and rituals and take seriously our intended outcomes, we also need to remain unattached to a specific outcome. There are many forces at play, and an outcome may not look exactly as you envisioned it yet may be exactly what you needed. Remain open to an outcome that feels different than expected but serves your ultimate well-being or even exceeds your expectations.

THE POWER OF SETTING INTENTIONS

When focusing your will toward a desired outcome of a situation or spell, it's important to clarify your intention. This means that you want to understand the motivation behind any spell.

For example, let's say that I'm struggling with insomnia and I decide to cast a spell to help bring on better sleep. I make a dream pillow with ingredients I understand help with insomnia and sleep. I add lavender, chamomile, and mugwort to bring calm and encourage deep sleep. But the next week, my insomnia is worse. What happened? I'm a powerful witch, so why didn't my simple sleep spell work?

Because I didn't stop to examine *why* my insomnia was so bad. When working with intentions, it is important to address the heart of the matter. If I'm struggling with insomnia because I'm worried about a conflict I'm having with a friend, I need to first address this conflict. I might cast a relationship mending spell and schedule some time to talk with my friend. Taking the necessary steps to address the root of the insomnia, my worry over the state of my friendship, will help my sleep and dream spell work better.

THE ROLE OF MANIFESTATION

Manifestation is the rigorous practice of bringing our intentions into reality through both practical and magical means. It is a muscle that must be toned. But how do we know it will work? Well, because we have practiced our principles of spellcasting and developed deep understanding of all of the ingredients. We have honored the wisdom of the natural world and those who have come before us. We can trust that our efforts will yield results because we have put in the work.

Manifestation is an important part of spellcasting. A daily manifestation practice will help your efforts yield the results you desire. This is where devotion and discipline come into your craft. Your daily practice can be very simple. Here are some tips:

Make a list of 10 herbs you want to learn how to incorporate into your witchcraft. Carve out 10 minutes a day to reflect on each herb, one at a time, until you can recognize and remember their unique properties.

Write a personal prayer or affirmation for protection and empowerment. Set aside one minute every morning to chant this affirmation to focus the energy for your day.

Place your tarot deck on your altar. Each morning after chanting your personal prayer or affirmation, draw a single card from the deck to reflect on during the day. This will help you learn the tarot and strengthen your ability to manifest your intentions.

Greet the day and the night. Each morning before you begin your day, take four deep and intentional breaths. With each breath acknowledge and give thanks to each of the elements: Earth, Air, Fire, and Water. Ask them to walk with, protect, and empower you through your day. Each night before bed, do the same, except ask the elements to ground, heal, and protect you in your sleep.

- Tend to your altars. Each morning burn a bit of dried mugwort and place a fresh glass of water on your altar to keep the energy clean and your guiding spirits and ancestors nourished.

The Witch's Wheel: Connecting to the Natural World

As you begin or continue your walk as a witch, it might feel a little overwhelming to trace all the significant intricacies and relationships within the natural world. Luckily, we can track natural resources and better understand their dynamics and cycles through something called the Witch's Wheel.

The Witch's Wheel (also called the Wheel of the Year) is a map and a calendar that can help you assess the timing of your rituals and actions. It will also deepen your relationship with magic and strengthen your spell crafting.

You'll learn the foundations of the wheel in the following text. Once you are familiar with the wheel's basic components, I encourage you to draw your own Witch's Wheel that includes your own important elemental, seasonal, and cyclical correspondences as well as significant dates and anniversaries for you. The Oracle Deck I co-created with Kiki Robinson, *The Living Altar Oracle Deck*, works intimately with the Witch's Wheel. I recommend picking up a copy to better acquaint your-self with this concept. In the meantime, here is an example of a wheel complete with a variety of correspondences. Use this as inspiration to create your own!

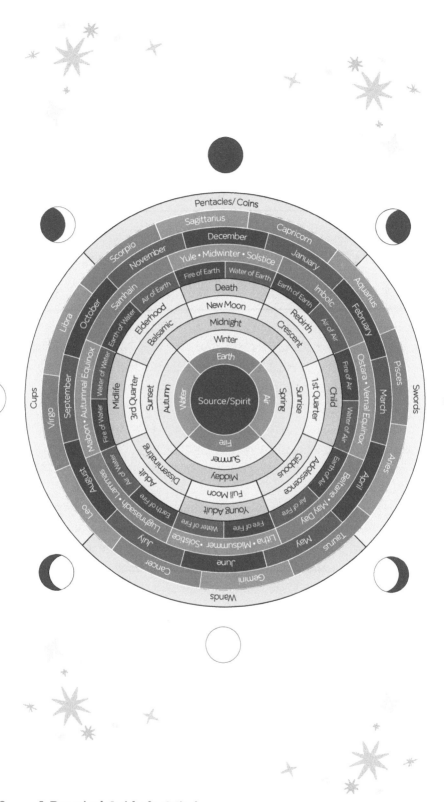

THE ELEMENTS

Take 20 minutes each day to reflect on the role of the Earth's elements within your life, spending 5 minutes with each element. Record your insights each day to enrich your craft.

Air is the element of insight, intuition, intention, and knowledge. Governing the mind, its magic lies in communication, thought, creative curiosity, intellectual pursuits, and higher consciousness. Air is a transitional element. It helps us define and align with our values and core beliefs.

Fire is the element most often associated with manifestation and transformation, as fire is both generative and destructive. Fire helps catalyze action by emboldening our choices. It also generates passion and feelings. Fire cannot exist on its own as it requires the air (intention feeds transformation) as fuel for change.

Water is the element associated with the changing of tides and shifting of circumstances. The magic of water is perpetual change, initiation, fluctuating emotions, and honesty. Water allows us to let go of what has been transformed by the fires of life and be open to new perspectives. Water is a transitional element that guides us to meet our edge and shape a new shore of it. Water helps us draw wisdom from what has been.

Earth is the foundational element in magic as it grounds our manifestations and intentions. Earth's magic is in resources, physical and sensory experiences, and relationships. Earth helps us define and affirm our boundaries and live up to our potential. Like boundaries, Earth is permeable yet firm; like relationship, it thrives from consistent tending and care.

The Elemental Source is the universal unity of all things. It is the primal essence from which all things arise and all things return. Sometimes referred to as the Void, it is the endless and unknowable expanse of potential that permeates and contains all life. It is a neutral source of infinite power and exchange. Some deify Source; I, however, see it as the silence between heartbeats and the stillness between breaths. It is godless and thus infinite.

THE SEASONS

The seasons align us to the bigger cycle of our lives. We can tap into the seasons to fuel life goals, connect more broadly to global and social energies, and plant the seeds for future advancements. We may also work with the cyclical regeneration of the seasons to bring healing to or channel energy from our emotional patterns. Go back a few years and think of a significant milestone in your life, such as falling in love, a breakup, or landing your dream job. Now draw to mind the season, month, and date of that event. Recall how you felt at that time. Slowly turn your personal Witch's Wheel forward year by year until you can begin to track the echoes of those milestones in each subsequent season. Notice the patterns of your life, season by season. These patterns can influence what you choose to do or manifest in the seasons ahead.

- **Winter** is the season at the beginning of the Witch's Wheel. It is the time to cull wisdom from past experiences in the anticipation of starting anew. Winter brings hope for the future.

- **Spring** is the season of regeneration. This season of new beginnings is the time to rebirth latent gifts and dormant ambitions and begin to realize the goals set during the quiet solitude of winter.

- **Summer** is the season of actualization, discovery, and a time to put into action the goals and lessons learned in the previous seasons. Summer is bold and almost reckless in its transformative ambition. A plan has been set in motion, and growth is inevitable.

- **Autumn** is the season of initiation, sacrifice, and purification. We have tended to our goals, relationships, and self-discoveries. Now is the natural period of shedding what didn't serve us, drawing inward, and winding down our momentum. It is a time to collect ourselves, reflect, and prepare for what's to come.

Solar Festivals

As the seasons shift, you can draw even more power through the relationship between the Earth and the Sun. These points of power are also known as solar festivals, which mark celestial rhythms. Creating ritual during these solar festivals is a perfect way to harness the immense power of a season for future workings. To learn more about traditional regional or cultural practices for these festivals, research folk customs associated with these festivals by your ancestral people.

- **Vernal Equinox** occurs at the halfway point between the winter and summer solstices (between March 19 and 21 in the Northern Hemisphere and September 19 and 21 in the Southern Hemisphere). At this point, the day and night become equal, and this moves us toward new possibility. This is when we harness the fullest expression of spring and embodiment of the element of Air. It's a time of inquiry, clarity, and ambition.

- **Summer Solstice** occurs at the halfway point between the vernal and autumnal equinoxes (between June 19 and 21 in the Northern Hemisphere and December 19 and 21 in the Southern Hemisphere). This marks the time when the day is longer than the night, which promotes dynamic transformation and growth. This is when we harness the fullest expression of summer and embodiment of the element of Fire. It is a time of great healing and outward expression.

- **Autumnal Equinox** occurs at the halfway point between the summer and winter solstices (between September 19 and 21 in the Northern Hemisphere and March 19 and 21 in the Southern Hemisphere). At this point, the day and night have equalized once again, which moves us toward decision and shifting inward once again. This is when we harness the fullest expression of autumn and embodiment of the element of Water. It is a time of sacrifice, gathering wisdom, and completion.

  Winter Solstice occurs at the halfway point between the autumnal and vernal equinoxes (between December 19 and 21 in the Northern Hemisphere and June 19 and 21 in the Southern Hemisphere). The night is once again growing longer than the day, which causes us to slow down and quiet the soul. This is when we harness the fullest expression of winter and embodiment of the element of Earth. It is a time of shadow working and reconciliation with past circumstances.

THE PHASES OF THE MOON

If the seasons align us to the bigger picture, the phases of the moon orient us to the intimate steps we take along our journey of the year. The lunar cycle helps us track the ebb and flow of energy on a day-to-day basis, providing guidance on breaking bigger projects and goals into more actionable steps. The lunar cycle also helps us gather, harness, release, and seed energies within our rituals. Here's how I work with the phases of the moon in my ritual and spell workings.

  New Moon. This is the first lunar phase, when the moon is between the Earth and the Sun. It is the petitionary phase of the moon—a reset. This is the time to seek guidance from Source, the elements, and your ancestors and guides, to begin a project, spell, or ritual, or to explore new intentions.

  Crescent Moon. This is when just a small sliver of the moon is visible. It is the clarity phase of the moon, ideal for gathering focus and defining your intentions. I see this as the final phase to set your groundwork before beginning your endeavors.

  First Quarter Moon. This is the time when we can see exactly half of the moon's surface. It is the gathering resource phase. You have clarified your intent; now is the time to harness the magic and begin charging your ingredients. Be sure to make offerings to your spirits and ancestors during this phase if you haven't already (see Working with Guiding Spirits and Ancestors, page 46).

Gibbous Moon. This is when the moon is more than half full, or "bulging." This is the "keys, wallet, phone" phase of the moon. You are getting everything ready to release your spell or perform your ritual. In preparation, sit in reflection, remember your intent, and release your attachments to the outcome.

Full Moon. This is the releasing phase of the moon. The Full Moon is when you complete preparation and release your spell or intent.

Disseminating Moon. This is when the moon begins cycling back toward a New Moon. This is when we remember that our choices and actions have impact. This phase of the moon flips the script. Up until now, you were enacting your intent. Now it is in the world and has begun enacting on you.

Third Quarter Moon. This when the opposite side of the moon is visible. This phase can have us feeling outside ourselves or slightly out of control (because we are!). We are being changed by the power of our enterprise taking up space in the world. Now is a good time to make more offerings to your spirits and ancestors (see Working with Guiding Spirits and Ancestors, page 46).

Balsamic Moon. This is when the moon is believed to be less than 45 degrees behind the Sun. It is the final and most restful phase of the lunar cycle. Now is the time to reflect and draw on your curiosity. How have you been changed by the work of this last cycle? What are the next steps needed to accomplish your greater purpose? This is the perfect phase for cutting cords with the past and inviting in the future.

Colors

The colors found in nature offer correspondences we can integrate into our magical practice. You can wear certain colors to draw the effects of those colors toward you or to embody the energy of those colors. You can also work with certain color candles or tools to focus your spell through the energy of that color. Noticing the colors you see during your day will help you better understand the impact of certain events. The following correspondences blend my Slavic culture with universal associations. Different cultures may have different associations with colors, so feel free to look into your own cultural associations and folklore to find associations that resonate with you.

- **Red**: passion, vitality, sacrifice, immediate action, fiery drive, protection, prosperity

- **Black:** groundedness, the cleansing and purging of energies, defense against ill will, protection, establishing boundaries

- **White:** healing, clarity, death, grief, mourning, knowledge, purification, the underworld

- **Yellow**: completion, harvest, wealth, abundance, success, progress; can also represent sickness

- **Blue**: the sky, far-sighted goals, calm, passivity, perspective, protection

- **Green:** fecundity, vibrancy, celebration, nature and its spirits; used to invoke governing and guiding spirits

- **Purple:** psychic energy, contentment, curiosity, lucidity; invokes dreamscapes

- **Gray:** ease, wisdom, mastery, neutralizing energy, oath breaking

- **Pink:** fidelity, friendship, softness and security, healing within a relationship

Divination, Tarot, Pendulums, Crystals, and Beyond

Divination is an umbrella term that refers to the seeking of information by supernatural means. Divination includes many mystical tools for the witch, such as the tarot, pendulums, crystals, plants, and even active visualization, movement, and breathwork.

Throughout this book, you'll find rituals that draw upon various methods of divination and inquiry. If you come across a ritual that calls for a tool that you don't yet have—such as a tarot deck—flip to the Resources section at the back of the book for further guidance.

Charms are another form of divination that is important for the witch's toolbox. A charm is a crafted object that the witch imbues with a specific energy—for example, a bundle of special ingredients tied up in a cloth and then carried or intentionally placed somewhere to generate energy around a particular intention like protection or luck. A charm can also be a short phrase that the witch sings or recites in order to invoke a particular state of being or raise energy for a particular outcome. A recited charm that I use often is one to ground and center myself: *Sacred are my breath, blood, bones, and worth. Bless me now, sweet Air, Fire, Water, and Earth.*

The Role of Spirits and Deities

While witchcraft is not a religion, many witches are theist, meaning they believe in a guiding sentient principle deity or some concept of universal source energy. For instance, I consider myself an animistic pantheist, and although I work with particular spirits, I believe that it isn't essential to devote yourself to any type of deity in order to be a witch. Here are a few forms of theism that are commonly found in witchcraft. Explore different beliefs to identify the role that the deification of nature might play in your personal craft.

- **Theism:** the belief that there are deities or supreme beings

- **Atheism:** the opposite of theism; the belief that deities do not exist

- **Deism:** the belief that if deities exist, they remain passive in our affairs

- **Gnosticism:** the belief in divinity that arises from a personal knowing

- **Agnosticism:** the belief that it is impossible to know if a supreme being or deities exist

- **Nontheism:** the absence of a clear idea or belief in the existence of a supreme being

- **Animism:** the belief that divinity exists in all forms of life from rocks, plants, and animals to the physical embodiments of the elements

- **Polytheism** (Paganism): the belief that many distinct deities exist simultaneously

- **Pantheism:** the belief in a supreme being that is in fact the totality of the Universe

- **Monotheism:** the belief that only one supreme being exists

- **Ditheism:** the belief in two equal but opposite supreme beings

Altars and Shrines

An altar is a sacred place where magic can gather and where you can place certain intentions and concerns in order to gain space from them. An altar is a home for spirit, an interface between the intangible and tangible worlds. We communicate with divine forces through our altars. Here are some types of altars I like to use in my craft.

- **Working Altars.** This is your everyday altar and is usually left up once built. My working altar is where I make my daily prayers and prepare and cast all of my spells and rituals.

- **Manifesting Altars.** These are separate altars built around a specific petition or desired outcome. I build manifesting altars when I'm working spells, offering prayers, or performing rituals to manifest blessings in a specific area of life, such as work, romance, health, money, or character.

- **Devotional Altars (or Shrines).** Shrines and devotional altars are like temples in your home. These altars are dedicated to honoring and bestowing blessings upon our helping spirits, ancestors, lost loved ones, deities, and greater beings. They exist as external focal points where you can deepen your relationship with the honored being through devotion.

CREATING YOUR ALTAR OR SHRINE

There are many different ways to build an altar, depending on the type of magic you practice and whether you're working with a specific deity or cultural tradition. Building an altar is a very intimate process. What you include on your altar, where you build your altar, and how you orient tools on your altar will take shape over time. Here are some tips to help you get started.

- **Altar Cloth.** This protects the surface of your altar and is a sign of respect to whatever your altar represents. Consider it the foundation of your altar's magic. I prefer to use natural materials for altar cloths such as vintage silk or cotton scarves, leather and animal pelts, large and flat pieces of bark or wood, or a simple square of cotton cloth.

- **Representation of Source.** At the center of your altar, place a candle or iconic object that represents your higher self, the part of you that is connected to the divine.

The Elements. Add items that help you connect to the elements of Earth, Air, Fire, and Water. You can emphasize one element over another depending on the focus of your altar. Place the elemental items in their corresponding direction around the center object.

- **Earth (North):** stones, crystals, wood, bones, soil, symbol of the pentacle, green

- **Air (East):** feathers, leaves, incense, empty dish, symbol of the wand, clear stones, yellow

- **Fire (South):** candle, red stones, herbs, plants, tarot cards, red

- **Water (West):** dish of water, grimoire, shells, mirrors, bells, blue

The Witch's Wheel. Your altar embodies a microcosm of the Witch's Wheel. For instance, you can place items that invoke the power of a particular season, such as flowers for spring or fresh fruit for summer. You can also place images of the moon to invoke a particular moon phase on your altar.

Offerings. I regularly leave offerings on my altar for the spirits and ancestors I call upon to assist my work. Living elements are nourishing for the spirits. You can add fresh water, flower, sweets, and any other goodies the spirits request whenever you feel called to do so.

Altar Maintenance. Break down and reset your altar every New Moon to keep the energy fresh and vital. Remove all remnants of previous spells and dispose of them once your rituals are complete. This allows fresh energy to enter into your life through your altar and prepare you to receive the benefits of your upcoming spell work.

Casting a Circle/Closing a Circle

Before working on any ritual or spell, take some time to center yourself and designate your space as sacred. A circle is an energetic boundary that defines and encloses the space within which your magical workings will take place. It is the veil through which magic travels. There are many ways to cast a circle. I will cast my circle through songs dedicated to the spirits, words of intent, and placing embodied elements on my altar. You can also trace a physical circle on the ground with chalk; carve a circle into the soil with your broom, staff, wand, or dagger; or create a circle with herbs, plants, or other ingredients. Here are some tips.

1. **Clear the energy.** You want to do a simple energetic clearing of yourself and your sacred space. Start by calling energy back to yourself from the people, places, and situations that have recently pulled energy from you. Let go of any energy you're holding that doesn't serve your higher purpose. You can also wash your hands and face in blessed waters to further purify yourself. To clear the energy in your space, light a candle and let the flame assist in burning out unwanted energy. You can also light incense to cleanse energy; powerful scents include rosemary, mugwort, and frankincense.

2. **Connect to your Intention.** Reflect on your intention behind the ritual or spell. Meditate on your relationship with your Source and channel your guiding spirits.

3. **Make final preparations** that are appropriate for your workings, such as building your altar, setting up your ritual or spell ingredients, chanting words of power, reciting your intentions aloud, setting up a meditation space, or changing your clothes. Once you're complete, begin to empower your intentions. Extinguish all candles and incense, unless your ritual calls for the candle or incense to burn completely down.

Maybe you manifested it, maybe it's your privilege.

Manifestation is a curious thing. I love what my dear friend Corinna Rosella from Rise Up Good Witch says about manifestation: "Maybe you manifested it, maybe it's your white privilege." That is to say, manifestation is one part intention setting, one part spell craft, two parts direct action, and five parts circumstance.

When working with the magic of manifestation, similar to working with intention setting, it's necessary to examine your social and political position in relationship to what you are seeking to attain. Be honest about your access to resources compared with someone with different access to resources or less privilege.

If your manifestations aren't unfolding in the ways you hoped, you may need to cast a spell banishing systems of oppression from your goal. I sometimes cast spells forgetting that as a trans non-binary femme, there are layers of energetic barriers I need to account for that a cisgender person doesn't. If you are someone who benefits from the privileges afforded you by our society (including your proximity to a white, cisgender, heteronormative, upwardly mobile, and able-bodied existence) and you consider yourself to be "really good at manifesting," I encourage you to pause to consider what else might be a factor in your success.

4. **Close the circle.** Once you're done with your spell, ritual, altar session, meditation, or magical working, release your attachments to the work. Be sure to thank the spirits who tended to your working, asking that they close all openings through which magic flowed into your ritual. Send all spirits home and open the circle you've cast in order to release the energy you've raised. If you cast your circle through prayer, you will release it through prayer. If you cast your circle by physically drawing or carving your circle, then you will erase what you've drawn. If you've traced your circle with herbs or salt, sweep up the material to use at a later date. Close out the connection to source energy that you established at the beginning of your work. Specifically ask all the spirits and energies you invited into the circle to leave and carry the magic into the world to serve your intention.

On Your Way

There is a saying that those with great spiritual knowledge and experience also carry a great responsibility. The work of the witch is as much about disrupting stagnation and shifting culture as it is about bettering our personal circumstances or aligning to the rhythms of the natural world. As you deepen in your path, you will be changed. As a result, your relationship with the world will change—and you might even change the world. You will need the proper tools to aid you on your journey.

3

GATHER YOUR TOOLS

A s with any craft, witchcraft involves some specific tools and ingredients. This chapter covers the foundational items you'll need to practice the spells and rituals that follow, from candles to oils, stones, and more. This is by no means an exhaustive list–there are many, many different ingredients and tools available, and every witch has their own preferences. I encourage you to play around and see what works for you.

Essential Tools and Ingredients

Following are my go-to tools and ingredients and their applications. Consider this a primer. As you try different items, record your experiences in your witch's journal. Take this information and build upon it in order to deepen your relationship with each tool, harness your power, and create your own unique toolbox.

HERBS

Herbs carry the sentience of the Earth and connect us to the living altar of the natural world. Whether freshly picked, dried, or store-bought, herbs are a staple of the witch's altar. When we enter into a relationship with plants and herbs, we connect to their magic on an ancestral plane. For example, when I add a bay leaf to my abundance oil, not only do I draw upon the magic of that individual leaf, I call upon every bay leaf to lend its power to my workings. And when I engage herbs significant to my ancestors, I tap into generations of rituals using those same herbs. Every herb corresponds to certain energies, but it's fine to make substitutions in your spells as you work through this book. If you can't find an herb that a spell calls for, think of the properties it brings to find a suitable replacement. Before working with an herb, familiarize yourself with its energy and ask for consent to add it to your spells.

If you want to stock your pantry, here are the herbs we'll use in the exercises in this book:

- Angelica root
- Basil
- Bay leaves
- Black peppercorns
- Juniper berries
- Lavender
- Mugwort
- Nettle
- Oat straw
- Patchouli
- Rosemary
- Willow leaves
- Yarrow

Essential Oils

The use of essential oils has grown more popular in recent years. These oils are widely available and offer a range of beneficial effects, from reducing stress to aiding sleep. They are called essential oils because they contain the most essential substances of the plant. Metaphysically, they can be thought of as the living essence of a plant and deserve to be treated with utmost care. Here are some tips to keep in mind as you work with oils.

- Never ingest essential oils! Distilled and bottled essential oils are 50 to 100 times more potent than their natural form. Even consuming one drop mixed in a bottle of water can cause severe damage to your digestive tract. Higher quantities can risk damage to major organ systems.

- Always add your essential oils to a carrier oil (a food-grade plant oil like olive oil or almond oil).

- Once it is mixed with a carrier oil, be sure to test the oil on a small area of skin first to make sure you don't experience any type of irritation or reaction.

- Remember that essential oils are very potent because they are concentrated chemical compounds. As such, a little goes a long way. When working with essential oils, less is more.

Here are the essential oils you'll find in the spells and rituals in this book:

- Bergamot
- Chamomile
- Clary sage
- Galbanum
- Hyssop
- Juniper
- Lavender
- Petitgrain
- St. John's wort

Tea and Tea Leaves

I remember growing up and having tea with my grandmother. She would read the leaves in my cup, helping me see patterns and shapes and deriving meaning from what we saw. The making and serving of tea is a ritual unto itself. Here are some ideas for using tea in your practice.

- Brew tea with herbs specific to the intention of your spell and drink in their wisdom as you write, research, and gather the ingredients of the spell.

- Read the leaves to determine if there is anything else you should be considering for your spell. A simple way is to prepare a cup of loose black or green tea while thinking about your inquiry. Drink the tea, leaving a small sip in the bottom of the cup. Swirl the liquid, place a saucer over the cup, and then flip the cup over on the saucer to catch the liquid. Peer into the cup and look in a clockwise spiral from the handle along the rim and into the cup. Look for obvious shapes and symbols made by the loose leaves as well as the negative space around the leaves. Trust your gut on the meaning.

- Blend a tea to match the intent of your workings and then bless and charge that tea on your altar as you prepare and cast your spell. Then drink the tea in the days following your spell to integrate it into your life.

- Brew a strong herbal tea and add to your bath to receive its healing power.

Incense

When you burn the physical body of the plant in the form of incense, it invokes a complete altar of the elements: Earth (plant), Air (smoke), Fire (ember), and Water (condensation and oils). As the plant burns, its spirit is released and carries your particular intention into the world. You can buy incense or make your own blends of loose incense, which you will mix with salt or ash and burn in a fireproof bowl. (For my All-Purpose Blessing Incense recipe, see page 54.) When you create a blend, write down your intention and burn the paper, then add the ash to your blend of herbs to help infuse it with your intention. I also think premade incense is a blessing! I burn herbal incense sticks on my altars as a daily offering to the spirits. I recommend all-natural, herbal incense cones and sticks; avoid chemically treated incense. You will need an incense holder as well as a dish to catch the ash.

Salt

I like to put sea salt on my altars as a symbol of abundance and to connect to ancestral magic. I can think of dozens of different uses for salt, from neutralizing energy to creating boundaries for spell work to cleansing, protection, and even summoning the dead. The beauty of salt is how culturally ubiquitous yet versatile it is. You'll use salt in many of the spells and rituals that follow, including adding Epsom salt to some ritual baths.

Plants and Flowers

You don't have to be outdoorsy or live deep in the woods to develop a relationship with the natural world. I live in a city, and my most cherished relationships with plants and flowers are with those I forage from our urban landscape. Regardless of where you live, cultivate deep relationships with the plants and flowers that grow around you. They will become your greatest allies in your craft, aiding in your spells and rituals, bringing grace to your workings, and connecting you to nature's greater powers. Place plants or flowers on your altars and incorporate them into your spells and rituals regularly.

Here are some of the plants and flowers we use in this book:

Apples

Carnations

Dandelion

Dill

Rhodiola

Roses

Stones and Crystals

I have always loved crystals, gems, and minerals. I bought and sold them for years when I owned a small metaphysical shop and have always found them resplendent and powerful. In my Slavic culture, it's common to wear crystal and stone beads to connect to the power of the land, as amulets for protection, or as talismans to bring good fortune. While many witches are drawn to crystals, the use of crystals in spell craft is not actually all that common. If you're compelled to work with crystals, keep the following things in mind.

- **The source and method of extraction.** Many crystals found on the market are a by-product of unethical strip-mining for other nonrenewable resources such as coal, gold, and lithium. These practices have devastating ecological and colonial impacts. Before you buy that rare and precious gem, ask where it came from.

- **Is this crystal necessary?** There are many ways to tap into energy of a particular crystal. Instead of buying a stone, you can connect to the magic of a crystal by meditating on its energy and connecting to it psychically through your relationship with the Earth.

- **Buy used and vintage.** Some people believe that crystals must be bought new in order to ensure that their energy is "pure." The truth is that crystals, like all sentient beings, have long and complex histories. Even if you buy a crystal "new" from the store, it has traveled a long way to get there. Buying used or vintage crystals and tools is perfectly fine and better for the Earth. You can cleanse their energy before working them, which I'll explain in more detail in chapter 5.

- **Borrow from the earth.** I like to collect rocks and crystals on my walks and adventures and, with their consent, work with them in my witchcraft and then return them to where I found them when the work is complete.

Some crystals to have on hand for the exercises that follow include amber, clear quartz, found stones, pyrite, and rhodochrosite.

CANDLES

Of all the tools necessary for the practice of witchcraft, candles are number one. I avoid scented candles because they usually contain chemical fragrances. Beeswax candles release more negative ions into the air when burning, so they have the extra benefit of purifying the air. However, they can be expensive and are taxing on the resources of our bee friends. Soy wax candles are a great alternative. Different types of candles we'll work with include votives, taper candles, tealight candles, and seven-day candles in various colors. Use a new candle for each specific spell you cast and allow that candle to burn completely. (This doesn't apply to altar candles, which can be used for multiple meditation and prayer sessions.)

There is so much to say about the practice of candle magic that entire books have been written on the subject. Here we'll focus on a few basic considerations.

- **Use specific blessings.** The trick to effective candle magic is in imbuing your candles with clear intentions. For instance, if you need support with money, you may want to do a candle spell for abundance, and it would make sense to choose a green candle (see Colors, page 24), surround it with coins and herbs or oils for abundance or prosperity, and set a clear intention for financial abundance. Now every time you burn this candle, your specific blessing is released to do its job in the Universe.

- **Stay focused.** I recommend working with one blessed candle at a time or many candles all blessed for the same intention. It is possible to pair different candles with different intentions at the same time, but it gets complex and requires a more advanced level of focus. I prefer to keep my candle intentions separate and work blessings one at a time.

* **Track your correspondences.** If you use color correspondences for your candle blessings, such as red for passionate love, pink for friendship, or gray for neutralizing potential harm (see Colors, page 24), or other types of meanings, such as methods of burning or candle preparation, be sure to record them in your journal to help inform your future candle work. The true magic of a correspondence is your belief in its power!

WAND AND STAFF

The witch's wand and staff are iconic tools for magic. Their purpose is to deepen the power of your spells and intentions. I ask my wand to hold and build strength around the intentions of a spell before I cast it. You can also use a wand to conduct energy during ritual or to open and close your circles. Some witches use a staff in a similar way. The staff can harness and direct forces of nature on a larger scale. I work with my staff to connect to the consciousness of Source and move the magic of the elements through me and into my ritual. The staff is a symbol of power. It can bind, seal, and banish energies and serve as a ward against harm. I also work with my staff when conducting group rituals.

I recommend harvesting your wand or staff from living trees or freshly fallen limbs and twigs. A wand should be no longer than your forearm, and a staff should be no taller than you. You can sand down and carve into your harvested tools or simply allow them to cure naturally. Some witches also work with iron, copper, or steel rods for staffs or wands due to their conductive nature. I prefer to work with willow, ash, birch, or oak. The wand and the staff are extremely intimate for the witch, representing their backbone, their connection to Source, and a means by which they conduct magical energy. For this reason, I advise against letting others work with your wand and staff.

MORTAR AND PESTLE

The mortar and pestle are a handy duo to have on hand. I see the mortar and pestle as the symbol of magic's simplicity and practicality. You can use them to grind herbs, plants, and petals. As you grind your ingredients, their power and energy are released into the mortar and pestle and can be tapped into for future workings. For many Slavic witches, the mortar and pestle are associated with Baba Yaga and represent our connection to ancestral magic and primal forces.

KNIVES AND SCISSORS

Knives and scissors are essential tools for any witch. Practically, we use them for cutting herbs, plants, fabric, and offerings, and mystically, we use them to sever energetic connections, carve out boundaries to establish sacred space, and carve sigils and symbols into the air and objects. You can also use the ritual knife similarly to the wand: to summon and direct elemental energies within your ritual. Your ritual knife can be a pocketknife, a letter opener, or even a fancy dagger. Unless you are following a specific tradition, it is really up to your tastes.

JARS AND VESSELS

You can't have too many jars, boxes, cloth bags, or vials on hand when you're a witch. I use jars to store my oils, herbs, teas, salts, soil, and other preparations and ritual items. I wash all of my jars with distilled vinegar before using them in order to clean them physically and energetically. (Be sure to use the appropriate cleaning solutions for boxes and vessels made of natural materials.) You also want to stock up on labels. Be sure to label each mixture with its name, ingredients, and the date you made the recipe or spell.

Witches also use bottles and containers to craft spells. As with candle spells, having a clear and specific intention is key. Here are some other tips:

- **Build it up.** When creating a contained spell or charmed bag, it is best to build it in layers. Start with ingredients that represent your motivation, then your intent, then your "fuel," followed by a catalyst, and then the intended destination or outcome. If you are taking a more elemental approach, add ingredients in the order of source, your intention, and then ingredients to harness Air, Fire, Water, and then Earth.

⁎ **Seal it.** Please put a top on it. And then seal it with wax. You can bless a candle to match the intention of your contained spell, burn the candle, and then allow the wax to drip over the lid of your jar or bottle and down the edges. If you are using a corked bottle or jar, dip the cork in wax a few times and then insert it into the vessel's mouth and drip more wax over it to seal it. Why seal it? You need your contained spell to exist as a closed ecosystem for as long as you desire the spell to be in effect.

⁎ **Store and let go.** When you build the witch bottle, the spell is alive and active until the vessel is broken. Once my spell is complete, I bury it wherever it makes sense to for the spell's intention to live. If it's a ward or protection spell for my home, I'll bury it near my front door. If it is a banishing bottle, I'll bury it someplace far from my home where I don't often go and where it won't be disturbed. Bury it and then leave. As long as the jar is intact, the spell inside will continue to work. There have been intact witch bottles found buried in the foundations of homes that are hundreds of years old! To break the spell, break the bottle.

MISCELLANEOUS TOOLS

Here's a quick cheat sheet of the tools you'll find mentioned in the spells, rituals, and exercises that follow. Before you get started, make sure you have most of these on hand (or can easily borrow from someone):

⁎ Basket

⁎ Bells

⁎ Coffee grinder (separate from your everyday grinder—meant to grind incense only)

⁎ Feathers

⁎ Fireproof bowl

Lighter or matches

Large mixing bowl

Mirrors

Nails

Paper

Pen

Shoelace

Spray bottle

Strainer, cheesecloth, or coffee filter

String

Stylus or straight pin

Wooden spoon

ADDITIONAL TRICKS OF THE TRADE

Here are a few more tools that I work with in my practice; feel free to add to them over time.

Voice. If you can name something, you can bring power to it or draw power from it. One of my favorite ways to do this in my craft is to sing about a spell or intention. You can also write, draw, dance, and use your breath to give something voice.

Cords. Cords, ropes, and braids help a witch harness and store energies during potent climatic, astrological, ritualistic, and seasonal events. By braiding, weaving, or tying knots into cords and ropes, we store the energy of a moment or an intention for later use.

Sigils and symbols. Sigils are images made up of various symbols that represent a complex intention in a single form. A symbol is a simple shape with a universal meaning (like a circle, spiral, triangle, line, dot, arc, or square), while a sigil is a complex shape derived from layering symbols to create a highly specific meaning (such as using five triangles and a pentagon to form a pentagram and adding a circle to make a pentacle). Sigils can be incorporated in your spells or used as a spell on their own.

Your Journal or Grimoire

People keep journals to track their memories, to help make sense of their circumstances, to clear their minds, to process situations, and to cultivate wisdom. Witches keep journals for all the same reasons. What makes a journal a grimoire is its focus on chronicling our journey in discovering and deepening in our craft. The witch's grimoire is a place to document ritual concepts, ideas for spells, tried and tested magical endeavors, recipes, charms, potions, and incantations. Like any of the witch's tools, its power is rooted in its affinity to the witch to whom it is dedicated.

GRIMOIRE BEST PRACTICES

Here are some practical tips for maintaining your magical grimoire.

- Your grimoire is a work in progress; it doesn't have to be perfect. Use it as a tool to track your learnings and let go of perfectionism. It's okay to scribble, cross out, and revise.

- Continue to modify. If you work on a spell or a ritual and upon casting again have a new realization, that is awesome. I call that "learning the craft." Continue to make new notes to your spells and grimoire as you build your practice.

- Ward your grimoire. Inscribe sigils and symbols that hold special meaning to you along the inside cover and page edges. Allow these symbols and sigils to protect your work, bring power to your spells and rituals, and contain the magic of your grimoire.

- Do not share your grimoire. I strongly recommend keeping your journal secret. This applies to your witchcraft as a whole: When it comes to spells, teas, potions, or charmed objects, never reveal exactly how you craft your wares. Always keep at least one ingredient a secret. I wrote this book as a practical guide to witchcraft, but even these spells are modified from my own personal practice!

You and Your Magic

The practice of witchcraft draws upon the power of our lived experiences more deeply than any ingredient. Because of this, you will be changed in the practice of magic. Here are a few last practical considerations for practicing your spells and rituals.

- **Frequency.** If a spell calls for repetition, repeat it. If it is a one and done, leave it be. If there is no specification, trust your instincts.

- **Adaptability.** If there's something about a spell that you don't connect with, reflect on why that is. What would work instead? Where many spell books intend for the caster to adhere to the specific instructions and ingredients, the spells in this book are all intended for you to adapt to your personal practice.

- **Integration.** Give yourself space and time to develop a personal understanding of each spell before performing it. Allow spells to integrate before moving on. Find pleasure in the subtlety of impact and cherish your growth. Who were you before the making of this ritual? During its casting? After it found its way into the world?

- **Belief.** Most importantly, allow yourself to believe in your work. Magic, like all crafts, requires patience, practice, and dedication. Keep an open mind, an honest heart, and a focused will.

Working with Guiding Spirits and Ancestors

A witch doesn't need to worship a deity or even believe in a supreme power, however, I encourage cultivating a mutually beneficial relationship with guiding spirits. These can be your ancestors—not only through your family of origin but also the ancestors of your social and cultural identities. As an example, I am from mixed Romani and Polish heritage. I do not know my ancestors by name, so I call to the spirits and "the grandparents" of my ancestral cultures instead.

As a trans non-binary femme, I also call to the trans ancestors and queer ancestors who walked this road before me. I also see the elements of Earth, Air, Fire, and Water as my ancestors. Remember: You do not walk this path alone. When identifying and building a relationship with your guiding spirits, be discerning. Not all spirits are helpful or want to support us. Even our ancestors and allied spirits will say no to certain requests! When working with a new spirit, vet it by asking questions about its nature and gauging your feelings about its answers. Spirits can be tricky. As with any relationship, it's important to have good communication, listen, and set clear boundaries.

When talking about working with spirits, it's important to also talk about cultural appropriation. Cultural appropriation, or the use of magic that is outside our cultural heritage, not only further marginalizes and harms others, it also makes our own magic oppressive. This is especially true when our access to the practice of other cultures is a result of our proximity to the privileges of a politically and socially dominant culture. When you're inspired by rituals, tools, ingredients, or spirits outside your culture, it's important to seek out the culturally appropriate counterparts within the traditions of your heritage. Check out the Resources (page 177) for more information.

Relating to Your Tools

Before moving on to the spells and rituals in the following pages, gather and spend time with the tools covered in this chapter.

What do you notice when you hold a wand compared with a ritual knife?

Can you sense the differences and similarities between mugwort, rosemary, and bay leaves? Gather a few candles of different colors and bless them with the energies associated with each color (see page 24). As you burn them, can you feel the difference in their energy?

Once you've spent time developing a relationship with a number of these tools, it's time to start practicing the spells in the following chapters.

HEALTH AND HAPPINESS

Now for the fun stuff! In this chapter, you will begin to apply all the foundations you've learned so far to the crafting and casting of spells. Specifically, you'll explore how witchcraft and magic can help you care for yourself. We'll focus on spells for your general health and happiness as well as the well-being of those close to you. Be sure to research the suggested ingredients for each spell and feel free to customize the rituals to fit your personal needs and style.

The Power of Self-Care

The care of self is a sacred ritual of devotion. The care of another, of community, is the temple where we practice this devotion. Take a moment to consider what self-care means to you. We all have different rituals that help us care for our deepest self. For me, self-care means getting enough rest, taking a long bath and anointing my skin with blessing oils, asking for help when I need it, and reaching out to a weary and heartbroken friend so they don't have to bear their burdens alone. It also looks like stepping up to assist my community in the ways that I am able. Self-care is as much about tending to our personal needs as it is about sharing our heart and resources with those around us.

Witchcraft Deepens Your Relationship with Yourself

Witchcraft gives us the power to be honest about who we are becoming. It also gives us a great amount of autonomy, which allows us to define who we are and claim our sovereignty. As we tend to our relationships with the natural world, our ritual tools, our spells, and our altars, we become more steadfast in our relationship with self. Witchcraft not only empowers us to be aware of who we are, it emboldens us to declare who we are not, who we never were, and who we will never be again.

Remember, magic has no affinity except to that which lives in the heart of the witch. The practice of magic is a faithless devotion, rooted in the heart. When we seek to reveal its power in our lives, it will without doubt reveal the truth of our own heart. This is what it means for a witch to "do the work." Reconciling what we discover with what we expected is a process of understanding ourselves. Once we begin to prioritize our relationship with ourselves, our values become clearer, our choices become more meaningful, and our actions have more integrity.

Spells and Rituals for Health and Happiness

The following are a mix of meditations, spells, rituals, recipes, witchery, and assorted conjurations to aid personal well-being, empower good health, and promote happiness. These exercises will vary in time and intensity depending on your needs. As an example, any exercise that asks you to reflect and process your feelings will take as long as it takes to get to the heart of the matter. Spells that require time to "cure," such as blessing oils, will take a specific amount of time. Good spell work is always worth the effort and the wait. Don't rush your rituals! Always allow time for integration after each spell and be sure not to "pick" at your castings once they have been released; instead give them time to unfold. If you aren't noticing a change in circumstance, that isn't an indication that the spell hasn't worked; it could mean that it just needs more time. Remember, spells build over time, and in order to cast one spell, you may need to prepare by working another ritual. As with all spells in this book, feel free to adapt these exercises.

Daily Protection Ritual

As a witch, it is vital to protect your energy. This prevents other energies and outside influences from disrupting your daily affairs. Daily protection spells also help keep unwanted spirits at bay. As you deepen in your witchcraft, you will grow more sensitive to energies and perceiving entities, and protection will become even more crucial.

Cast this spell in the morning before starting your day and in the evening before going to bed. Do this even if you do not leave your home.

candle

matches or lighter

2 tablespoons dried
    mugwort

fireproof bowl for burn-
    ing herbs

olive oil

small dish of sea salt

small bell

1. Recite the following prayer:

   I call upon the sacred and sovereign elements of creation and the spirits who guide and protect me in my life and craft. Come to me. Protect and cleanse me. Lift and carry from me, my work, and my altar any thoughts, spirits, energies, or beliefs that would not benefit me or my workings this day. Assist them to places they can serve and be served well. Beloved spirits, elementals, and guides, clear all unnecessary distractions and obstacles from the path before me. Open the ways of magic to me that I may serve and be served in good ways. Remember me and help me be remembered in good ways. May my intentions, actions, and values align in all that I do. May I receive all of the blessings intended for me with ease and grace. May all ill will cast toward me miss its mark and return to Source. And so it is.

2. Light the candle and envision its light filling you with the magic of Fire. Will the flame to clear all blockages within you and return them to Source. Repeat this phrase three times:

   Sacred Fire, cleanse, empower, and protect me. And so it is.

3. With your matches or lighter, light the mugwort. Allow the smoke to surround you.

Envision the fragrance clearing your mind and thoughts. Repeat this phrase three times:

Sacred Air, cleanse, empower, and protect me. And so it is.

4. Pour a small dollop of olive oil into your palm. Rub your hands together and pass your oiled palms over your body. Apply the oil to the top of your head, your heart, the nape of your neck, and the bottoms of your feet. Invite the oil to form a protective bubble around you. Repeat this phrase three times:

Sacred Water, cleanse, empower, and protect me. And so it is.

5. Next, take a pinch of sea salt and cast it in a circle around you. Invite the earth to fortify your boundaries and fortify your bubble of protection in all directions. Ask the sea salt to pull all the blockages deep into the Earth below you to be cleansed and returned to Source. Repeat this phrase three times:

Sacred Earth, cleanse, empower, and protect me. And so it is.

6. Ring your bell in the four directions—North, South, East, and West—to honor and release all the elements.

7. Complete the ritual by extinguishing your candle. Allow the protection spell to remain active throughout your day and while you sleep.

All-Purpose Blessing Incense

I enjoy making my own ritual herbal incense blends. It is very easy and inexpensive. You can use this technique for any herbal incense you wish to make–simply change up the listed herbs to match your intention. The following recipe is my go-to herbal incense. Burn it daily to support your well-being. You can also add it to charmed bags for extra protection and to bring blessings to your intentions. A little goes a long way.

large mixing bowl

wooden mixing spoon

1 tablespoon basil

2 tablespoons rosemary

petals of 9 carnation flowers

1 tablespoon willow leaves

2 tablespoons lavender flowers

2 tablespoons angelica root

3 bay leaves

1 tablespoon mugwort

1 tablespoon yarrow

coffee grinder (dedicated to processing incense only) or mortar and pestle

jar and label for storage

1. Call in a protective circle and place all of your ingredients around your mixing bowl.

2. Call in the elements and helping spirits one by one. Consider using the prayer from the Daily Protection Ritual (page 52).

3. Hold each herb in your hands. Notice their energies, invite their magic into your ritual, and ask permission to make use of their magic in this incense. Offer gratitude. Envision the four elements moving through your hands and into the herbs. Ask the elements to empower each herb and infuse it with your intentions. Add the herb to the bowl.

4. Once you've added all the herbs to your bowl, mix them together, envisioning their energies blending together. Repeat the following as you do:

By wind and rain, through sun-drenched soil, you've come to join me here. I lift my heart and share my altar. Bless me and the path I travel.

5. Allow the magic of the elements to continue to move through you. When your work feels complete, spoon the mixture into your coffee grinder or mortar or pestle and grind the mixture into powder.

6. Spoon the ground mixture into your labeled jar. Place on your working altar to charge for at least three days.

7. Thank the elements and helping spirits, release your prayer, and conclude your ritual. You can repeat this ritual of preparation to craft any herbal incense.

Note: Here are the main properties of the different herbs used in this ritual.

Basil: summons personal guiding spirits and governing spirits of nature, promotes wellness, opens intuition, offers protection

Rosemary: cleanses and protects your psychic energy, promotes focus

Carnation Flowers: wards against all forms of malignancy

Willow leaves: promotes wellness, deepens connection to spiritual powers

Lavender flowers: soothes the spirit, calms the mind, activates psychic power, promotes intuition, connects to the power of dreams

Angelica root: wards against curses, connects to ancestral power

Bay leaves: clears the way for blessings—you can even write words of blessing and protection on each leaf

Mugwort: activates inner magic, connects to the magic of Source, offers protection, opens psychic nature

Yarrow: promotes healing, cleanses energy fields, removes negative energies

All-Purpose Ritual Oil

Ritual oils—also called anointing oils—come in handy for blessing spells, charm bags, and tools. The crafting of a ritual oil is a spell in itself—the simple act of preparing it will welcome its intended energies into your life. Keep in mind that oils take a while to cure, so if you need an oil for a ritual or spell, plan ahead and prepare it a month in advance. (You can always substitute an incense blend if you don't have a ritual oil on hand, although the elemental properties are different.) I prefer to use a mix of fresh and dried herbs, essential oils, minerals, bones, and ash from written prayers. You will find a rhythm to making your own oils. This recipe uses the All-Purpose Blessing Incense (page 54), but you can use any incense depending on your intention.

fireproof bowl

white votive candle

an acorn or chestnut

small clear quartz

2 tablespoons
  All-Purpose Blessing
  Incense (see page 54)

glass jar

pen and paper

matches or lighter

7 drops of each
  essential oil:

• hyssop

• galbanum

• bergamot

• juniper

sunflower oil

strainer

bottle for storage

4 cups Epsom salt
  (optional)

1. Place your ingredients around the fire-proof bowl.

2. Recite the following enchantment:
   Air above, Earth below, Fire within, Water around. With gratitude, I call the elements to this altar. Clear and open the paths of blessing before, within, behind, and all around me. Devour any energy maligned against me, and ward me against all harm and any energies that distract me from my purpose. Transform these energies into blessings of protection for my body, spirit, and mind. May this be so with ease and grace. So it is.

3. Light the candle. Envision each element blessing your ingredients one by one.

4. Place the acorn or chestnut, the quartz, and the incense in your jar.

5. Reflect on the nature of blessing, safety, protection, and boundaries. Using your pen, write these reflections on your piece of paper, and then place the paper in your fireproof bowl. Light the paper and watch it burn in your bowl. Once the ash has cooled, add it to your jar.

6. Add 7 drops of each essential oil to the jar.

7. Next, fill the rest of the jar with sunflower oil. Put the lid on the jar and shake it while reciting the preceding enchantment. Place the jar in the bowl.

8. Let the candle burn down. Close your ritual space.

9. Allow the oil to cure for at least one lunar cycle.

10. After a complete lunar cycle has passed, strain the herbs from the oil. Pour the oil into the bottle, add the quartz stone, and store.

11. Dispose of the herbal ingredients as an offering to the spirits. You can also add them to 4 cups of Epsom salt to use as a blessing and protection bath.

Note: Begin this oil at the New Moon and let it cure until the next New Moon.

Ritual Bath Salts for Empowerment

Ritual baths are a staple for self-care. Not only do they relax you and leave you feeling amazing, they are powerful cleansing and empowerment rituals. A ritual bath will detoxify your physical, emotional, and energetic bodies. A blessing ritual bath will charge you up with the energies specific to the intention of your bath. For this ritual bath recipe, we'll use the All-Purpose Blessing Incense (page 54) and All-Purpose Ritual Oil (page 56) we made earlier, but you can use any incense or oil blend that calls to you. I hope it is clear just how many ways you can build your spells by layering various rituals and preparations around the same intention.

large mixing bowl

black votive candle

1 cup Epsom salt

1 cup sea salt

2 tablespoons
   All-Purpose Blessing
   Incense (see page 54)

1 ounce All-Purpose
   Ritual Oil (see
   page 56)

wooden spoon
   for mixing

large glass jar

1 to 2 ounces honey

1. Call in the elements and helping spirits one by one. Consider using the prayer from the Daily Protection Ritual (page 52).

2. Place your ingredients and offerings around the mixing bowl.

3. Light the candle. Envision each element blessing your ingredients one by one. Add the salts, then your incense, and then your oil to the bowl.

4. Use your wooden spoon to blend these ingredients. As you mix them together, envision the ocean and its vast power filling the bowl. From tide pools to the deepest seas, call the living ocean to your altar.

5. Place your candle in the middle of the bowl of salts, light it, and let it burn down. Let the wax spill over the top of your salts. As it does this, it will seal your spell, giving boundaries to the ocean it contains.

6. Remove the wax remnants. (You can save them as offerings or, if they are beeswax, you can mix them into your salts.) Pour your salt into your large glass jar for storage.

7. When complete, close your ritual space, and gift your offering of honey on your altar to nourish your guiding spirits. After two days, remove the honey and take it outside to give back to the elemental spirits.

8. Add ¼ cup of this salt mixture to a hot bath whenever needed.

Protection Candle

When you need a bit of magic but don't know what kind of spell to cast, blessing and burning a candle is a simple and powerful choice. Candle spells are among the most creative and flexible spells on the witch's altar. You can customize a candle to fit any purpose or intention, and a candle can contain an entire spell. Here is an easy blessing ritual to make a protection candle.

white pillar candle and
  container
pen and paper
fireproof bowl
matches or lighter
1 tablespoon
  All-Purpose Ritual Oil
  (see page 56)
7 drops juniper essen-
  tial oil
pen or stylus
1 tablespoon
  All-Purpose Blessing
  Incense (see page 54)

1. Invoke sacred space for the intention of blessing this candle for protection.

2. Reflect on the idea of protection. In your mind, come up with a list of at least four words that embody this reflection.

3. Chant those words until you deeply connect with them. Envision the shape of each word. Then use your pen to draw these shapes on the paper.

4. Try different combinations of the four shapes until you find one that makes one cohesive shape. This will be your sigil (see page 43) that embodies protection. Draw this shape on a fresh piece of paper.

5. Place the paper with your sigil on it in your fireproof bowl. Light the paper and allow it to turn to ash.

6. Pour your ritual oil into the bowl and add 7 drops of juniper essential oil. Stir together.

7. Use a pin or stylus to carve your sigil into your candle, imbuing it with the power of protection.

8. Now, rub the oil and ash mixture onto the candle, chanting the list of words that you used to create your protection sigil. Focus on your sigil as you massage this oil and ash into the candle.

9. Lastly, roll your candle in your blessing incense and set in its container to cure on your altar for at least 24 hours.

10. Light the candle and reflect on its illumination anytime you need a boost of protection.

Inner Altar Meditation

Inside each of us exists an altar through which our magic moves and on which our spells churn. It is where the witch gathers resolve and fortifies their relationship with themselves and their craft. Our inner altar is a place where we can go to access our ancestral selves, draw up our inherent wisdom, communicate with our magic, and harness energy from our elemental nature. This meditation uses scrying—a form of divination that utilizes natural elements such as water, fire, smoke, and crystals as conduits to insight—to access your inner altar. By gazing into their own living elements, a witch can access all the information they need.

candle
Mason jar or tall glass
  container
matches or lighter
bowl of fresh water
hand towel

1. Invoke sacred space. Place the candle in the jar, light it, and set it in the middle of your bowl of water. Find a comfortable seated position and place the bowl and towel in front of you.

2. Set your intention to journey within yourself to find and connect with your inner altar. Take 10 intentional breaths. With each inhalation, draw your personal power and sovereignty to you. With each exhalation, release any doubt or uncertainty into the candles flame to be transmuted into power and sovereignty.

3. Dip your hands in the water and wash your hands and your face, clearing any energy or thoughts that might prevent you from accessing your inner altar. Allow the candle flame to transmute this energy into a fully illuminated path toward your altar.

4. Dry your hands and face with the towel. Soften your eyes and gently gaze into the reflection of fire on water. With each breath, allow the path inward to become more illuminated. Now you are scrying with water and fire to discover your inner altar.

5. Follow the sensation of movement inward toward your inner altar. Now imagine a sanctuary of some kind, a room or place in nature, deep within you. Enter into this sanctuary.

6. Invite your inner altar to emerge at the center of this sanctuary. Approach your altar, noticing what you can about its nature. Are there items on this altar? Is there anything distinct about its shape, its energy, the way it's set up?

7. When you are ready, ask your inner altar for an item that you can place on your outer altar to help connect them. Once that item clarifies itself, thank your altar and begin your return journey.

8. When you fully return to the present moment, wash your hands and face again. This will break the reflection on the water and help you fully emerge from your meditation and close the pathway to your inner altar.

9. Extinguish the candle and gift the blessed water to your ancestors on your altar. Leave the water on your altar overnight and then dispose of it either by feeding it to your houseplants, pouring it into a vase to nourish fresh flowers, or gifting it to the trees outside.

10. Once you have practiced this technique enough, you will feel more confident to connect to your inner altar without the external ritual of scrying by water and flame.

Energy-Cleansing Ritual

This exercise builds off the Inner Altar Meditation (page 62). It will help you draw upon the vital forces of terrestrial and celestial source energy and wield it in your day-to-day workings. It will also guide you in creating a protective energy shield. I recommend doing this ritual at the beginning and end of your day as well as after any particularly charged experience. Be careful not to maintain your shield for too long, as it can be energetically draining. However, you can pulse your shield throughout the day like mini sonic blasts to break up any harmful energies that may be accumulating around you.

1. Begin by invoking a sacred space. Activate your inner altar with the Inner Altar Meditation (page 62). Once you have found your inner altar, make an intention to draw upon source energy through your altar.

2. Imagine that you have energetic roots that descend from your altar deep into the Earth and branches that ascend up into the celestial realm.

3. Allow these roots and branches to connect you to the most perfect and sovereign source of terrestrial and celestial energies. Draw these energies to your altar and allow them to form a sphere around your intention.

4. Invite them to continue feeding this sphere as they ascend and descend, respectively, until they form an energetic circuit.

5. In this gentle circuit, imagine the sphere at your altar growing and expanding until both you and your altar are within it. Continue to draw upon celestial and terrestrial source energy until this sphere expands to fill your entire body.

6. Allow the sphere to gather and push out of you any non-self and stagnant energy. Invite the sphere to gently expand until it pushes through and begins to surround your physical body.

7. Allow the sphere to gather and push away any non-self and stagnant energy from around you. Imagine this sphere expands beyond you until it reaches 24 feet in diameter.

8. Invite the source energy that feeds this sphere to transmute into a shield of protection around you.

9. Under this shield allow a protective membrane to form around you. Allow this membrane to gather strength from the sphere until it feels like there is pressure forming around you.

10. Imagine swiftly expanding the membrane in all directions, shattering the shield, rapidly scattering the pieces outward from you in a psychic sonic burst. Allow this burst to clear harm and any unnecessary obstacles from your path.

11. Allowing the sphere of source energy to remain, draw the shield back in until it rests comfortably on your inner altar.

12. Draw your roots and branches inward back from the terrestrial and celestial source.

13. Allow the sphere to slowly dissipate throughout the day. Repeat this ritual as needed.

Note: You may be noticing intriguing sensations, such as spinning, dissolving, hollowness, or temperature shifts. Don't be alarmed. This technique grounds, clears, and protects you. Ask yourself how long it has been since you experienced this level of grounding, clearing, and protection. Rather than shrinking away from the sensations, expand into them and trust that your ritual is working.

Elemental Pentagram for Harnessing Power

We are elemental beings. We are animals. We are part of this world. This exercise, which draws inspiration from the Wiccan invocation of the pentagram, helps you connect to your elemental nature. Here, you'll use your body to invoke a pentagram of the elements. Tune into your own body to determine which element is associated with which quadrant of your body. You can also incorporate the Energy-Cleansing Ritual (page 64) to create a sphere around you. I like to bring amber into this exercise for its additional healing properties, but you can use any healing stone, bone, or herb that calls to you.

piece of amber or other healing item

1. Invoke sacred space. Lie on your back and arrange (or imagine) your body in the shape of a star. Place your amber or other healing item on your chest. Take a few grounding and centering breaths.

2. Bring your breath and attention to your head. Imagine that your head is connected to the compassionate source of all creation. Draw this source energy to your inner altar and allow it to empower your sovereignty.

3. Now, bring your breath and attention to the lower right quadrant of your body. Imagine that the lower right quadrant of your body is connected to the compassionate source of the element of Earth. Draw its magic to your inner altar to empower the Earth within you.

4. Bring your breath and attention to the upper left quadrant of your body. Imagine that the upper left quadrant of your body is connected to the compassionate source of the

element of Air. Draw its magic to your inner altar to empower the Air within you.

5. Bring your breath and attention to the upper right quadrant of your body. Imagine that the upper right quadrant of your body is connected to the compassionate source of the element of Fire. Draw its magic to your inner altar to empower the Fire within you.

6. Bring your breath and attention to the lower left quadrant of your body. Imagine that the lower left quadrant of your body is connected to the compassionate source of the element of Water. Draw its magic to your inner altar to empower the Water within you.

7. Repeat four times, projecting this pentagram into your healing object.

8. Deactivate the pentagram by releasing the elements in the opposite order than you invoked them. Close any energetic portals opened for this exercise.

9. Release your sacred space and place healing object on your altar until you need it next.

Wellness Brew

Working with herbs is a wonderful way to tend to the wellness of your physical, emotional, and energetic bodies. While many herbal recipes are simple, please remember that there are a number of precautions to take when it comes herbal medicine. It's always a good idea to consult a clinical herbalist before trying new herbal remedies. Please take time to do additional research to learn about potential contraindications, side effects, and drug interactions when it comes to ingesting herbs. While it's true that anyone can work with herbs and practice herbalism, only those with supervised clinical experience are considered clinical herbalists. This is a very important distinction because as herbalism and witchcraft continue to rise in popularity, so do the risks of misinformation spreading. The good news is that I am a clinical herbalist! The following recipe should be relatively safe and beneficial for most people. As with any substance you consume, you must do your own due diligence to confirm that it is safe for you. This Wellness Brew is a general tonic to support your body's physical, emotional, and spiritual immunity.

3 tablespoons dried
   nettle leaf
2 tablespoons dried
   oat straw
2 tablespoons rhodiola
1 tablespoon dande-
   lion leaf
quart jar or
   French press
wooden spoon
large square of cheese-
   cloth or coffee filter

1. One by one, bless each herb and place it in the jar or French press.

2. Next, fill the jar with room-temperature water and stir the herbs together using your wooden spoon.

3. Place the container with the herbs and water in the refrigerator. Let the mixture steep for 3 to 4 hours.

4. Strain the herbs from the water using your cheesecloth or coffee filter. (You can compost the used herbs.)

5. Immediately refrigerate the brew, and drink and enjoy it throughout the day. This brew has a shelf life of less than 24 hours (including preparation time), so you want to try to drink the full quart in one day. Dispose of whatever you can't finish.

6. Drink a quart of this brew a few times a week or daily if you're in a particularly stressful period.

Note: Do not use a metal spoon for this preparation as it may cause the herbs to oxidize faster, resulting in a spoiled flavor.

Daily Insight Tarot Spread

The tarot is one of the most accessible and relevant tools of divination. Anyone can draw insight from the tarot, no prior experience needed! All you need is your own deck. It's okay to read the cards for yourself, cross-reference tarot books, and learn the meanings of the cards as you go. The tarot has many rich layers that you'll discover over time, but at first just let it be simple and intuitive. If you ever get stuck in your exploration of the tarot, seek out a professional to read for you and teach you. Mentors are a wonderful way to deepen your craft. That being said, here's a simple insight spread that I use as a daily forecast.

tarot deck of your choosing

1. It's best to pull this spread after you've finished your daily clearings and protections. When your mind is clear, shuffle your deck and invite it to embody the day that lies before you.

2. Once the deck connects to the potential of your day, set it on your altar. Next, you will ask three questions, pulling a card for each question as a response from your day. Pull three cards, asking:

   How can I best support my physical body today?

   How can I best support my emotional body today?

   How can I best support my spiritual body today?

3. As you pull them, lay the cards faceup from left to right. Reflect on them for a few moments, allowing your impressions of each card to settle in. Make note of the symbolism of the card, anything you might know about the meaning of the card, and how each card makes you feel. Record your impressions of the cards' answers.

4. Allow these answers to guide how you plan and approach your day. At the end of your day, revisit the reading and make notes about any moments or milestones in your day that felt particularly significant or closely aligned to the tarot spread.

5. Shuffle the cards back into the deck.

Conclusion

Take some time to reflect on what you learned in the casting of these spells and the working of these rituals. Make notes in your grimoire. What modifications would you make the next time? Every time we cast a spell, we are changed and our relationship with our inner altar deepens. It is important to document your progress and track your feelings and intuition. Take a moment to draft a few rituals and spells of your own for health and happiness. Draft a ritual or spell to empower any aspect of your relationship with self-care.

5

FAMILY, FRIENDS, AND COMMUNITY

This chapter reveals how witchcraft can help us deepen the magic of our relationships, honor our integrity, and command our sovereignty. Witchcraft can reveal subtle truths about ourselves and our loved ones. The spells and rituals that follow will empower you to face your relationship patterns, address issues, and bring more accountability to your connections with your friends, family, and community. Relationships require some of the deepest work, so please be gentle and diligent in your practice, tracking and tending to your desires and revelations with care.

The Importance of Relationships

Our relationships with ourselves and others provide rich life experiences. These experiences challenge us, open us, lift us up, dismantle our false beliefs, shatter our illusions, and support us in cultivating a more genuine sense of self. Our relationships nurture the blessing of becoming, providing ample opportunities for self-actualization. The work of the witch, even the solitary witch, is rooted in the power of relationship.

I'm not someone who believes that things happen for a reason, nor do I believe we always have a choice in what happens to us or even how we respond in the moment to certain situations. I do believe that challenging relationship experiences provide an opportunity to tend to our relationship with ourselves. I find this to be a helpful perspective when tending to any relationship within my life.

The lessons our relationships provide serve as catalysts for personal and collective growth. When we talk about the intimate magic of relationship, keep in mind that we aren't just speaking about romance. We are talking about the sacred connections we forge with our friends, our guiding spirits, the ancestors, our coworkers, clerks at the market, our family, our neighbors, members of our community, even those with whom we are in conflict—and, of course, ourselves.

Through *all* of our relationships we learn more about how to navigate boundaries, consent, mistakes, trust, betrayals, misunderstandings, compassion, empathy, and kindness. We learn to discern hurt from harm and disparities from discrimination and heal past and future wounds through reconciliation. The energy of our relationships impacts us in unknowable ways. They are vital to our health, happiness, and well-being.

How Witchcraft Can Help You Heal Wounds and Strengthen Relationships

Witchcraft can guide you in healing wounds or resolving the impact of harmful interactions. This is a key component to anyone's life because humans are deeply social by nature. This doesn't mean that we all love big crowds or parties or that we even all enjoy meeting people. But companionship and mutual understanding with other beings are a salve for even the most introverted person. We need connection to thrive, be it the company of a trusted friend, a support group, family, a counselor, or an animal companion. The magic in this chapter will help support various types of relationships, including love relationships and those with your family, friends, and community.

FAMILY

Family can be a beautiful and often complex altar in and of itself. Family doesn't always mean relatives by blood either. Family, especially for a queer and trans witch like myself, can also mean a safe, trusted group of friends. The magic of family is that it helps us tap into our ancestral roots and conjure deeply intimate initiations. I view family as the operating system that is running inside us at all times. It often needs upgrades, and sometimes it is so outdated that it needs to be wiped and completely replaced. Magic helps us become aware of these operating systems so that we aren't inadvertently playing out faulty family patterns in other relationships. It can also help us interrupt harmful patterns and replace them with beliefs and actions that align with our individual values.

FRIENDS

Friendship is where we get to practice the truth of who we are without the constraints of familial conditioning. Even in friendships that feel familial, we are freer to be ourselves. The magic of friendship is that it is a relationship by mutual choice and respect. It is rooted in the present and supports who we are now and who we are becoming. Friendship is a great harmonizing force in our lives. The altar of friendship is where we go to be seen, hyped up, called to task, and witnessed, and where we are held accountable for our goals. Friendship, when done right, breeds integrity.

LOVE

Love is a trickster god. There are as many expressions of love as there are relationships in life. No two people can love you the same way, nor can you love everyone in your life the same way.

Love is mercy, grace, an unearned gift, and a faithless devotion that will not be contained by any one definition. It is all too easy to confine love to the normative definition of a binary romantic partnership. Yet love is available to us through every single relationship we tend. This is the singular beauty of the miracle of love. Its altar is without border, without binary, and without label and cannot be controlled.

COMMUNITY

The witch is most powerful in service at the altar of their community. We aren't meant to walk through this world alone, yet many of us feel so alone. Finding our place in the world can be challenging for many different reasons, but tapping into a larger collective does wonders for any witch. I'm not saying we need to stage elaborate public rituals or build a huge social media following in order to foster community—the work can be much subtler than that. For instance, for any ritual or spell you perform, you can include an invitation for its outcome to be of benefit to the greater collective and any being who needs it. I do this even when I'm offering healing spells and prayers for myself. When I show up to my work grounded in my sovereignty, clear in my boundaries, and aligned with my values, I am more able to engage in my relationships with respect and integrity.

Using Your Powers for Good

Magic can't solve all our problems or make all our hopes come true, but the practice of witchcraft *can* clear the way and give us support as we access the appropriate resources. Even the most powerful spells will fall flat without real-world efforts to assist in their blessings. For instance, if you cast a spell to address a sore muscle that's been aching for days but aren't administering any physical interventions like taking a pain reliever, applying ice or heat, resting, or stretching, the pain will likely persist. Don't use your magic as a Band-Aid or to prove false beliefs right. Magic requires practical measures to generate meaningful impact.

I also don't believe in casting magic to bend someone's will for personal gain (such as casting love spells on someone to make them love you—it's not love if you have to force it!). But you can cast spells to sweeten the energy that exists between you and another person to help foster the growth of the relationship. Relationships will follow their destined course, but you can support the health of a relationship with magic and see what happens.

On the flip side, I do believe in the casting of defensive and offensive magic when someone causes me harm, particularly when unprovoked. This is especially relevant for people who are marginalized and whose identities have been politicized by dominant social structures. For many of us, magical self-defense remains the only recourse we have. Magic is indiscriminate, like the forces of nature. Whether magic is "good" or "bad" is determined solely by what lives in the heart of the witch. It is up to you to learn your limits and establish what you will and won't do with your craft. Hexing or cursing isn't wrong; sometimes offensive magic is the best and only defense we have in life. Before you consider a magical intervention, take an inventory of the situation and consider other actions you may want to take first:

- Have you cut energetic cords with the situation and the person?

- Have you cast protection and boundary spells? Have you tried to banish the situation or the person instead?

- Are you tending to any culpability you have in the situation?

Be wise, practice within your capacity, be honest, ask for help, be accountable, learn, and grow.

Spells and Rituals for Your Relationships

The following are an assortment of spells, rituals, meditations, and suggestions to help you tend to the health of your relationships. Their focus ranges from cutting energetic cords, to opening yourself up to intimacy, to conflict resolution and ways to support community. As always, take what works for you and expand on it to suit your goals and cosmology.

A Relationship Inventory

You'll notice throughout this grimoire that I talk a lot about tracking intentions and motivations and acting within your value system. These considerations help us remain honest and act with integrity. If our actions are out of alignment with our values, we need to either adjust our values to accommodate that action or change our behavior to accommodate our values. When we know where we stand, we can better show up to ourselves and one another. This exercise will help you take an honest look at the current state of your relationships. Remember, where you stand is where you begin, but it may not always be where you stay! It's perfectly reasonable to change as you learn and grow.

paper and pen
candle

1. Invoke sacred space and light your favorite candle.

2. Reflect on the following questions and journal your responses. You don't have to do everything in writing. Lean into your own creative style and journal through drawing, movement, song, and imagination.

   When, where, and under what circumstances do I feel safe and at ease in relationships?

   Where do I feel unsafe and uneasy in relationships?

   Where am I open to communication and feedback in my relationships?

   Where is it challenging for me to communicate or receive feedback in my relationships?

   What character traits do I value in a friend?

continued ⇗

A Relationship Inventory *continued*

    Can I identify any actions or beliefs I bring to my relationships that contradict my core values or perpetuate obstacles?

3. Review your responses and list out any character traits or themes that emerge. Allow these to define your values.

4. Next, separate your values into two categories: those that are nonnegotiable, about which you are not willing to be flexible or collaborative, and those that are negotiable, about which you are willing to be flexible and collaborative within the context of a relationship.

5. Blow out your candle. Revisit this exercise as often as you need to.

Spell to Summon Your Witch's Familiar

A witch's guiding spirits walk with them in known and unknown ways. Some may have even walked with the witch since birth, although the witch may not be aware of it. These spiritual allies tend to reveal more and more about themselves to a witch over time. The most intimate type of guiding spirit (besides ancestors) is the witch's familiar. This is a familiar spirit that assists witches in their craft, often intercepting magic on the witch's behalf. Some believe that the fate of the familiar is aligned to that of the witch they are serving. So, for better or worse, what befalls the witch befalls the familiar—meaning they are one of the few spirits that truly have our best interests at heart. This ritual will help you connect to your familiar as mentor. Before you begin this spell, write a list of qualities you would like in a mentor that upholds your values.

black taper candle

symbol that represents you as a witch

list of values pulled from your Relationship Inventory (see page 81)

dish of sea salt

1 teaspoon rosemary

1 teaspoon mugwort

1 teaspoon lavender

matches or lighter

fireproof bowl

4-inch-by-4-inch square of black cloth

6 inches red ribbon

biodegradable offering for your familiar

1. Invoke sacred space and place your candle, symbol, and values list on your altar.

2. Add the rosemary, mugwort, and lavender to your salt dish and mix them together.

3. Sprinkle half of this mixture around the candle to invoke a circle of protection around you. This protective circle will repel deceptive spirits and attract your true and sovereign potential.

4. Light the candle and slowly recite the following spell at least nine times; repeat as often as needed throughout the spell:

To the one who has walked with me since birth, who knows my many names. I call to you through time and space. Reveal yourself to me. Our fates align and our wills find solace in each other's company. Familiar mine, reveal yourself to me.

continued >

5. Burn your values list, blend the ashes with the remaining salt and herb mixture while reciting the preceding spell.

6. Spoon the mixture onto the middle of your black fabric square. Gather the four corners of the fabric, imbue each of them with one of the four elements, and summon your familiar spirit with the power of the elements.

7. Securely tie the bundle with the red string and place on your altar to charge as the candle burns.

8. Once the candle burns down completely, collect the herb and salt circle to use in a ritual bath/shower; within 24 hours.

9. Carry your bundle with you as a talisman to connect you to your familiar. Take note of any dreams you have at night or signs you notice during the day. Don't force your familiar to reveal itself. You will know when it arrives.

10. Leave your offerings in nature as a gratitude to your familiar.

Cord-Cutting Ritual

Cords are tendrils of energy that are created when an emotional charge connects us to another person, place, or circumstance. These connections can be platonic, sexual, developed over long periods of time, or sudden. Cords are natural but aren't always necessary, mutual, or helpful. Tending to your energetic cords is essential in maintaining your energetic hygiene. Cutting cords with someone won't cause them to leave your life forever, but it will give you space to make more autonomous choices about that relationship. You can pair a cord-cutting ritual with relationship mending, rituals to stop gossip, or even banishing spells as a way to focus your intentions for healing.

9 inches string (in any color that represents the relationship)

matches or lighter

fireproof bowl

1. Invoke sacred space.

2. Tie a knot in one end of the string to represent you and one on the other end of the string to represent the other person. Tie a knot in the middle of the string to represent the relationship.

3. Bring to mind the relationship and cord you want to cut. Imagine that you and the other person are both clouds of light.

4. Envision the energetic cord between you. Where does it connect on or within each of you? Observe how the colors of each of your clouds moves through the cord and into and around each of you.

5. Hold the string in your hands. Call your energy home to you by pulling your cloud toward you through the cord. Send the other person's energy back to them by pushing their cloud toward them through the cord.

6. When you are ready, place the string in the fireproof bowl, light it with your matches

continued ›

Cord-Cutting Ritual *continued*

or lighter, and release the cord to the fire. Collect the ashes of the cord in the bowl.

7. Repeat this ritual every night for the next three nights. On the fourth night, collect all the ashes and scrub your body with them in the shower or bath.

8. I recommend working the Ritual for Forgiveness (page 91) to help you integrate the cord cutting.

Spell for Broken Hearts

Conflict can be an uncomfortable, if necessary, aspect of growth in our relationships. Conflict in relationship, especially friendship, doesn't feel good. This is a spell to mend broken hearts and relationship rifts. Perform this spell when you are in conflict with yourself, a friend, a lover, or even family. It may be helpful to perform a Cord-Cutting Ritual first (see page 85). This spell draws on sympathetic magic, enacting through ritual what you want to see happen in the world around you. You'll use sweet and sticky things to attract and bind things to you and cut something sour to banish conflict.

paper and pen
apple
knife
large plate
few fresh flowers of
  your choosing
jar of honey
tealight candle
matches or lighter
3 pennies

1. Invoke sacred space, set up your altar, and arrange your ingredients.

2. Clarify your intention by writing down your side of the conflict on a piece of paper. Be accountable, address culpability, and try to see the other side as well. Identify any opportunities for apologies or changes in your behavior for future progress.

3. Hold the apple in your hand and reflect on the relationship you're seeking to sweeten. Think about the conflict you are trying to mend. Pour into this apple the energy of the situation in totality. When you are ready, visualize the current separation between you and the other as an opportunity for growth.

4. Cut the apple in half across the middle to reveal a star. Place the apple halves on the large plate.

5. Arrange the flowers on the plate in a circle around the apple halves, strengthening your relationship bond so it can hold this conflict and resolution.

continued >

6. Hold the honey jar in your hand and envision sweetness between you and the other person; imagine its stickiness bringing you closer together in order to resolve this conflict.

7. Pour the honey over the apples and within the circle of flowers.

8. Place the candle between the apple halves to signify the power of your relationship and the illuminating journey of healing between you. Light it up!

9. Allow the candle to burn down completely, transmuting the energy of conflict into healing wisdom.

10. When complete, take all the organic ingredients and release them into a beautiful place in nature or compost them. Leave the 3 pennies under a tree near your released ingredients as offerings to the spirits.

11. Finally, after the spell settles, make a date with your friend with the intention of talking through and resolving the conflict. Better yet, do this spell together with your friend!

Honoring Self-Friendship

We often lean into our friends for encouragement, support, and companionship. Friendship is a sacred ritual and an ancient salve for the heart. We give so much to our friendships—sometimes without even realizing how much energy we are giving. This is why when tending to our friendships with others, we must also tend to our friendship with the self. This ritual will help you honor your most sacred friendship, the one you have with yourself. I recommend doing this at least once a year on your birthday. You can also modify this ritual as a birthday gift for your friends or after a conflict with a friend as a way to mend the bond.

large bowl filled with fresh water
tealight candle
large glass jar with lid
3 fresh flowers with stems removed
poem or blessing of your choosing
matches or lighter

Note: Duplicate these ingredients for every person who is involved in the ritual if you choose to offer this in the company of others or as a gift for a friend.

1. Place the bowl of water in the center of your altar. Place your flowers in a triangle around the bowl and the tealight candle and jar on either side of the bowl.

2. Recite the poem or blessing as an invocation of sacred space.

3. Gather the flowers and speak a word of blessing into each:
   The first flower is a blessing for where your friendship with self has been.
   The second flower is a blessing for where your friendship with self is now.
   The third flower is a blessing for the future of your friendship with self.

4. Place the flowers into the bowl and stir the water while reciting your poem or blessing as many times as you need to connect to its power.

5. Charge your tealight candle with the energy of adventure, opportunity, and growth you want to experience in your friendship with

continued ⇗

self. Light the candle, inviting the illumination to further bless the water. Let it burn completely.

6. Pour the water into the jar, close it with the lid, and let it charge on your altar for 1 week. Offer the flowers and any remaining water to the spirits.

7. At the end of the week, bathe or shower with the water from the jar to help you integrate the ritual.

Ritual for Forgiveness

I am not someone who forgives just for the sake of it–I believe that forgiveness is healing only when it is sincere. However, I do believe that I can take actions to ready myself for forgiveness. Forgiveness is an ongoing conversation with yourself, your history, and your past narratives. It is a ritual of transmuting past impact into a clearer path forward. Forgiveness unfolds much like understanding, much like a relationship. It first requires a willingness to look at the situation and be honest about your experience and your feelings. This ritual is an invitation for forgiveness, a spell of preparing yourself to both forgive and receive forgiveness.

candle
matches or lighter
paper and pen
13 inches red string

1. Reflect on the circumstances around which you are seeking forgiveness. Think about all aspects of the situation without judgment or blame.

2. Invite a conversation of forgiveness into your mind and heart. When you're ready, light your candle.

3. Release the energy of that situation to the candle flame. Envision the energy being transformed into an energy of forgiveness.

4. Answer the following questions:

   What have I learned about myself from this situation?

   How can I tend to the hurt caused by this situation?

   What is my relationship with forgiveness in regard to this situation?

   Is there anything about this circumstance that I need to apologize for?

continued >

Ritual for Forgiveness *continued*

5. If you are in need of forgiveness, write an apology letter. If you are in need of an apology, write a letter of forgiveness.

6. Rip up the pages and tie the pieces together with the string.

7. Bury the bundle under a tree and ask the Earth to help you grow from this situation.

8. Follow through with any conversations and action steps necessary.

Ritual Bath for Intimacy

Intimacy is a state of deep, vulnerable connection with yourself and others. It is the act of showing your true nature to another without censorship, apology, or expectation. Your capacity and desire for intimacy might be very different than others. This is perfectly okay. In fact, it is beautiful and sacred. Every relationship presents new opportunities to discover and cultivate intimacy. This ritual bath will help you prepare for intimacy and invite it into your relationships. If you don't have a tub, a shower will also work.

2 tablespoons dried
   mugwort
fireproof bowl
matches or lighter
black seven-day candle
white seven-day candle
red seven-day candle
bouquet of orange
   flowers
1 quart goat's milk (can
   substitute coco-
   nut milk)
All-Purpose Ritual Oil
   (page 56)
jar of honey
mixing bowl

1. Invoke sacred space and draw a bath.

2. Place the mugwort in the fireproof bowl and light it. Disrobe and bathe your body in the smoke. Allow it to cleanse and open your body and heart as an invitation for intimacy.

3. Next, light your candles. Allow the flame of the black candle to absorb any intimacy blockages and transmute them into receptivity. Allow the flame of the white candle to transform any ancestral patterns that may be holding you back from intimacy. Allow the flame of the red candle to fill your heart with the invitation and stretch you into your full capacity for intimacy.

4. Pluck the flowers from their stems and cast their petals into the bath, blessing the water with beauty and tenderness.

5. Add the milk to your bath in order to nourish these blessings and soften your body to absorb the blessings.

6. Anoint your body in your ritual oil and speak words of affirmation as you rub it into your skin.

continued ⟩

Ritual Bath for Intimacy *continued*

7. Step into the bath and pour the honey all over your body. Massage the honey and oil deep into your skin.

8. Soak in the tub. Slowly massage the water into your skin and begin to wash away the excess honey and oil.

9. Bathe in this delicious bath for as long as you need.

10. When your bathing ritual is complete, gather the flower petals into a bowl and set them outside the tub; then drain the tub. Gift the blessed flowers to the helping spirits by returning them to nature.

11. Blow out your candles and close your circle.

Return to Sender Spell Bottle

We've all participated in gossip in one way or another–either as the victim of gossip or the perpetrator (or both). People know that gossip doesn't feel good, and yet it still continues within friend groups, communities, schools, workplaces, and just about anywhere. But gossip is an insidious way to pit us against each other and distract from our shared need for mutual support and community. Here is a simple witch bottle spell to stop gossip and to repel negative energy.

paper and pen
nail (try to find one
   in your house that's
   been used before)
jar with a secure lid
small mirror
juniper berries
1 tablespoon dried
   rosemary
secret ingredient of
   your choice
fireproof bowl
1 tablespoon dried
   mugwort
matches or lighter
white taper candle

1. Invoke sacred space. Place your ingredients on your altar.

2. Gossip spreads. Although you might not know its source, you can still address its wave. This spell follows this echoing wave back to its root.

3. On your piece of paper, write the following spell (feel free to modify the words):

   I return to Source the root and impact of all gossip and negative energy directed toward me; intentionally and unintentionally. I banish all falsehoods, lies, and harmful words cast against me. May anyone who gossips against me forget my name. May any energy directed toward me with the intention of harm to my body, spirit, mind, character, work, or reputation be returned to its source. May my blessings be unobstructed, I receive my blessings with grace. So it is.

4. Fold this paper three times and place it on your altar.

5. Hold the nail in your hands, and draw into it the energy being directed toward you. Envision the nail being driven into a dead tree thousands of miles away from you. Drive the nail through the folded paper and place both in your jar.

continued ⟩

6. Hold the small mirror and imagine all the harmful energy and gossip being reflected by this mirror back to its original source. Then place the mirror in the jar.

7. Hold the juniper berries in your hand and ask their support to cleanse and protect you from present and future gossip. Place the berries in the jar.

8. Hold the rosemary in your hands. Allow it to clear your mind of any negative belief or thought that has risen from the energy and gossip being directed toward you. Place in the jar.

9. Add a secret ingredient and securely place the lid on the jar.

10. In your fireproof bowl, burn the mugwort and ask it to clear any lingering residue of this negative energy from you.

11. Light your candle and drip the wax all along the lid of the jar to seal your spell. Allow the candle to burn down.

12. Bury this jar in a dead tree far away from your home and leave offerings to the spirits of that place in gratitude. Do not break this jar! It will continue to protect you against all forms of gossip for as long as it is intact.

Blessing for Friends and Family

Though it is appropriate to offer blessings and prayers for the health, well-being, and safety of those we love, I advise against making specific prayers for another person without their consent. How can we know what's best for another person? What is best for another may be outside your comfort zone or in opposition to your belief systems. It doesn't really matter what I want for another person. My priority is supporting those I love in finding whatever they want for themselves. In that spirit, here is a general blessing I like to make for my family and my friends on a daily basis.

Take a few intentional breaths to center and ground yourself. Repeat this prayer over and over again until you sense a shift in your own connection to self.

I call upon the virtue of Air to open the ways before those I love so they may access with ease that which offers them inspiration.

I call upon the passion of Fire to illuminate the ways before those I love so they may access with ease that which offers them healing.

I call upon the wisdom of Water to transmute the ways before those I love so that they may access with ease that which offers them comfort.

I call upon the boundaries of Earth to enrich the ways before those I love so they may access with ease that which offers them kindness.

May the grace of the ancestors walk with me and those I love. May all my loved ones walk in the grace of this blessing and find themselves remembered well. May we all do well with what we remember.

Altar for Community

Community is so valuable, and yet we can easily take it for granted if we aren't mindful. Community magic is about sharing resources and making a collective effort to help ameliorate the stress on one individual person. You can build this altar with your community as a means of healing, grounding, and honoring its power. You can also build this altar to serve as a beacon to receive a safe invitation into a supportive community. As with all other petitionary spells, it is important to also make clear and actionable steps to bring your petition into life.

altar cloth

2 tablespoons dried
   mugwort

fireproof bowl

matches or lighter

5 taper candles (white,
   red, or black)

small feather

single flower

small shell

small stone or bone

paper and pen

small box (big enough
   to fit the preced-
   ing items)

1. Lay down your altar cloth and envision strong roots for a healthy community.

2. Place the mugwort into the fireproof bowl and light it. Allow it to smolder, cleansing and blessing your altar as you build it.

3. Next, place a candle in the center of your altar to represent your community's connection to Source and mutual values. Light this candle.

4. Place the remaining four candles on the outer edges of your altar to invoke a sacred container for community and charge them as follows:

   a. East: Invites Air and its gifts of inspiration, knowledge, curiosity, and communication to be present and honored within your community.

   b. South: Invites Fire and its gifts of passion, power, healing, joy, and transformation to be present and honored within your community.

c. West: Invites Water and its gifts of wisdom, counsel, initiation, and transition to be present and honored within your community.

d. North: Invites Earth and its gifts of boundary, relationship, fortitude, and resource to be present and honored within your community

5. Place the following objects around the center candle to hold the gifts of the elements.

a. Place the feather in the east.

b. Place the small flower in the south.

c. Place the small shell in the west.

d. Place the stone in the north.

6. Light your candles and write your petition and blessing for community.

7. Fold up the paper and place it in the box. Set the box on your altar.

8. After the candles have completely burned down, gather the altar items and place them in the box along with your petition. Sprinkle the ashes of the burnt mugwort in the box as well.

9. Dispose of the remnants of the candles that have burned down. Wrap this box in the altar cloth and place it somewhere on your working altar or in a safe place to continue to generate energy for your community.

Conclusion

Magic challenges us. As we cast spells and perform rituals, our perceptions of self can change. It is our responsibility to tend to the ways we have changed and the ways we aspire to grow. As we discover more about ourselves, it's vital that we tend to any impact these discoveries have on our relationships. What kinds of rituals and spells are needed to help you tend to your relationship with self and others at this time? As we change and grow, so do our relationships. And often, so does our environment. So now let's spend some time tending to our intimate spaces and the sacredness of our homes.

MAKE YOUR HOUSE A HOME

Home is a sanctuary. Everyone deserves a safe place of their own to rest, heal, relax, be themselves, and retreat from the outside world. Yet sadly, not everyone has access to this basic human right. As you work the spells in this chapter, direct your intentions to help everyone have access to the blessing of a safe home. It's also important to approach the rituals in this chapter with the understanding that our experience of home growing up can shape our present experience of home, for better or worse. Be gentle and responsible with any memories that surface for you as you work through these pages.

The Significance of the Home

For the witch, home is a temple within which we honor our most intimate relationships. Home isn't just a physical dwelling place. It can also be a sense of belonging, an answered calling, a point of reference, or a hope or desire that begs for realization. When we think of home, we may also think about where we have been, the path that led us to this present moment, and all the ways we've learned to name ourselves along the way. Home can be our origin story, our chosen family, and our community. If we think of home as simply a place, we miss the point. Home truly is where our heart is. The work of the witch is to call our hearts home to where we stand and send the magic of what we stand for into the world.

HOW YOUR HOME AFFECTS YOU

Our physical home can hold the energy of those who have lived there before us. Its walls, floors, and ceiling can channel memories of the land on which it stands and the elements from which it was built. When I tend to my home, I offer blessings and ritual to make healing spaces for my history, my ancestral self (the parts of me that have been), and the history and ancestors of the land where my home sits. When we speak of our nonphysical home, or the sense of home that we find within, memories may surface by association as you tend to the different places in your home. For example, if as an adolescent you struggled with self-esteem and processed your frustrations in your bedroom, you may experience an overlay of past struggles as you process present-day frustrations in your bedroom.

Every home has a spirit. People often feel like someone or something is haunting their home. Usually this is psychic and energetic residue from the previous tenants or the history of the land. While history cannot be changed, you can do clearing work to change the charge of a specific energy. Sometimes after performing a clearing you may still perceive a presence—this is likely the spirit of the home trying to communicate. Try to listen and honor them. Most of the time, they want nothing from us except a mutually beneficial cohabitation.

Understanding the Energy of the Home

I view the home as a sentient being, with each room within holding a unique aspect of its personality. When tending to your home, it is important to understand the role each room plays in the overall health of the home as well as the nature of your relationship to each room. For example, I will always see the kitchen as the heart of my home. My most powerful memories of childhood live in the kitchens of my grandmothers and my mother. No matter what else was going on in my life, the kitchen was always a safe place. On the flip side, living rooms have always been a challenge for me. Even when living alone, it takes great effort for me to feel at ease in the living room. You, however, may feel that your living room is the heart of your home, and so it is! When we understand our affinities for certain spaces, we can better support the health of each room and empower its role in maintaining the overall well-being of our home. We will also be able to discern when our memories and personal histories are disrupting our sense of wellness within certain areas of the home. Here are some basic considerations to keep in mind when it comes to the main rooms of the house.

THE KITCHEN

The kitchen is often a very active place in the home and functions as your upper digestive system functions—processing energy in nourishing ways for the overall body. I perform most of my spells in my kitchen and favor the kitchen for abundance and healing work. The kitchen is where I remember to show up to myself, nourishing my own needs first so that I may nourish others from a place of integrity. It is a place where I can practice the best of myself while also giving my best to others. The kitchen generally has a community aspect to it, with people coming and going and congregating to prepare or share meals. The energy of the kitchen is active and generative.

The Bedroom

Your bedroom is the holiest place of your home. Its energy is dedicated to your heart and your dreams. It is sacred. How you keep your bedroom has the most intimate and direct impact on your personal energy, so you want this room to be inviting, organized, calming, and a sincere reflection of who you are. When cleaning the house, it's best to start in the bedroom, the most inner sanctum of your temple, and work your way out to other rooms. This ensures that the energy of your home is calibrated to serve your deepest dreams and desires. Refrain from keeping active spells in your bedroom as they may interfere with your sleep and your dreams. My favored workings for the bedroom are those pertaining to intimacy with self, lovers, healing of family patterns, personal empowerment, intentional dream work, and creativity and inspiration.

The Living Room

The living room also holds the energy of community and can empower us to tend to the health of our relationships. It can be thought of as the nervous system of your home—its energy empowers us to connect with others, to our work, to our traditions, and to ourselves. Living rooms invite us to pause and process the impact of things we experience in our day-to-day lives. The living room is also a place to honor our ancestors. It is customary for a witch to keep an altar to their ancestral and cultural spirits in a prominent place in the living room. I also tend to the altar of my house in the living room. The house altar is a place to ground the energy of your home and can be used to connect all of the other altars of your home.

THE BATHROOM

The magical energy of our bathroom can be harnessed to empower our sense of self and help us release and transmute energetic blockages in our lives. The bathroom is also one of the few places we can fully disrobe, soak in the bath or shower, cleanse our bodies, and pause to look at ourselves in the mirror. The bathroom's energy can be the most challenging for people because of the depth of intimacy it conjures. Try to treat the challenge of the bathroom as an initiation, or a house of mirrors, where you will come to know yourself on a deeper level. The bathroom is an altar of transformation and purification. In the chamber of this altar, we have an opportunity to bring illumination to our most shadowed selves. Rituals for the bathroom include those of daily purification and protection, deep cleansing, self-respect, ritual baths, and spells to collect our obscured and abandoned selves.

Spells and Rituals for a Peaceful, Comforting Home

The following are an assortment of spells, rituals, and potions to help you tend to the energy and overall well-being of your home. We'll work with cleansing rituals, guardian spirits, wards for protection, creating a house altar, blessing your home, and more. Feel free to modify what you find here to suit your needs and your particular place of dwelling.

Simple Cleaning Potion

Adding blessed herbs and oils to your cleaning products is a timeless and simple ritual to support the overall spiritual health and hygiene of your home. Whenever you physically clean your house, it's a great opportunity to energetically cleanse it as well. Make cleaning potions in advance to have on hand. I charge my clearing oils at the Full Moon and my blessing herbs and oils at the New Moon. Customize the potions for your home by whispering your intentions into dried mugwort, burning it in a fireproof bowl, and adding the ashes to your cleaning solution. You can use a spray bottle or cleaning basin for this ritual. I prefer using a spray bottle because it's easier to use and store. Once your potion is ready, clean away!

spray bottle (or cleaning basin)

one to three from each category of these charged essential oils:

- juniper, rosemary, thyme, mugwort (for clearing and protection)

- orange, rose, dill, lavender (for blessing and healing)

1 teaspoon dried mugwort

fireproof bowl

matches or lighter

distilled vinegar (optional)

1. Gather your supplies and clarify your intentions.

2. Fill your basin or spray bottle with water.

3. Add your oils. The more essential oils you add, the less of each you'll need. Select one to three oils each for clearing and blessing. Avoid direct skin contact with pure essential oils and wash exposed skin with soap and water.

4. Gather the dried mugwort into your hands and speak your intentions for the health, blessings, cleansing, and protection of your home into the herb. Ask that it carry these intentions throughout your home.

5. Place the mugwort in the fireproof bowl and light it. Gently blow the mugwort until it smolders. Use the smoke to cleanse yourself before you begin your cleaning rituals. Add the mugwort ash to your cleaning solution and stir.

6. For an extra disinfectant, I like to add a few tablespoons of distilled vinegar to my solution.

Happy Gnome, Happy Home

Every home has a guardian spirit; in Slavic culture, we call them the Domovoi. These spirits tend to the health and well-being of a home and everyone who dwells within it. Perform this ritual once a month in the kitchen at the New Moon to nurture and honor your guardian spirit.

tealight candle

6 inches red string

small bell

large metal mixing bowl

matches or lighter

1 apple

knife

small bowl of cream

bowl of sweets, like
  sugar, honey, or candy

1. Create your altar by placing the candle, string, and bell in the large mixing bowl. Light the candle.

2. Slice the apple across the middle (not top to bottom) to reveal a star and place the halves around the altar along with the bowls of cream and sweets.

3. String the bell with the red string while reciting this spell:

   I call to the powers of Earth and Fire, Air and Water: Bless these offerings in honor of the one who protects and serves this home. To the guardian spirit of my home, I thank and honor you for the seen and unseen work you do. May the elements lift and bless you. May these offerings nourish you and may the night protect and guide you. My blessings upon you, sweet friend, come and feast. Whenever this bell rings, I will turn my gratitude to you. May your hearth be blessed with health, safety, love, and wealth in equal proportions to those that bless mine. So it is.

4. Reflect on these blessings as the tealight burns down.

5. Tie the bell to the handle of your stove and close your ritual container.

continued >

6. Place the apple halves and bowls of cream and sweets into the metal bowl and set it on your stove overnight. In the morning, gift the cream and sweets to the land outside your home or compost them. (Never flush offerings down the drain.)

Window Wards

This ritual uses sigils (see page 43) on your windows as wards for your home. This is a very simple spell of protection. You can refresh these wards after each cleaning; they may change over time, so keep a record in your grimoire. I tend to reuse and cycle through particularly potent wards for a while. For an added boost, add extra clearing and protection wards at the New Moon and extra blessing and healing wards at the Full Moon.

paper and pen
clean rag
1 cup Simple Cleaning
  Potion (see page 108)

1. After cleaning your home, reflect on the energy within your dwelling. What additional energy is needed to support the well-being of your home at this time? Write down a single word of affirmation that describes that support.

2. Reflect on the state of the four elements within your home. What gifts do they offer to support the well-being of your home at this time? Write down a single word of affirmation that describes these gifts.

3. Write down a single word of affirmation that describes the energy of blessings and protections you wish for your home

4. Next, look at your three words and identify the most prominent shape in each word. For instance, if your words are "love," "sovereignty," and "joy," the most prominent shapes are the "v" of "love," the "g" of "sovereignty," and the "y" of "joy." Write the three shapes in a line next to each other, modifying them as desired.

continued ⟩

5. With your pen, layer the shapes on top of each other until they form a larger cohesive shape. This will become your sigil. You will know when you have it because the shape will click in your mind.

6. Once you have this new shape, envision all the words it contains. This charges the new shape as a sigil.

7. Dampen your rag with the Simple Cleaning Potion and draw this shape on all the outward-facing doors and windows of your home. Imbue the sigil with the energy of all your affirming words as you work. Repeat as often as desired.

Doormat Warding

After energetically and physically cleaning your home and working your wards, it's a good idea to add this extra bit of protection under your doormat. The intention is to cast off unwanted energies as you enter your home and invite in only welcome energies. This is a very simple Cottage Witch spell and should be replenished every time you clean. Feel free to use whatever herbs call to you.

large mixing bowl

wooden spoon

Measure out the following ingredients for *each* external door of your home:

- ¼ cup sea salt
- 1 teaspoon crushed black peppercorns
- 1 teaspoon dried yarrow
- 1 teaspoon of dried nettles
- 1 teaspoon of juniper berries

1. Invoke sacred space and gather your ingredients.

2. Bless each ingredient with the intention of protecting your home and casting away any unwelcome or negative energy.

3. Blend all of the ingredients together in your mixing bowl and stir with the wooden spoon. Connect to the elements of Earth, Air, Fire, and Water, and ask them to bless these herbs with their protection and magic.

4. Go to your front door, lift up the doormat, and drop your salt mixture directly on the ground in front of your door. Do this for each outside door of your home.

5. Using the handle of your wooden spoon, draw an X with arrow points on each of the four terminations. While you draw this X and arrows, focus on casting away any disrupting energies.

6. Next draw four arrows in the open quadrants created by the X. Draw these arrows pointing toward the center of the X. As you draw these arrows, focus on inviting in energies that support the wellness, abundance, and safety of your home.

continued >

Doormat Warding *continued*

7. Next draw a square around these combined shapes. This square represents a psychic and energetic boundary that will serve to protect your home.

8. Place the doormat over the salt. Refresh these doormat wards every time you clean your home.

Blessing Bundles

One of my favorite ways to bless the home is by making bundles of natural materials that I gather on walks. A blessing bundle can serve as a living embodiment of a prayer or intention. It's a good idea to make new blessing bundles every season to welcome the power of that season into your home and more fully align your home to that phase of the Witch's Wheel. You can also make blessing bundles anytime to hold the power of a particular intention such as peace, clarity, emotional wellness, spiritual protection, or even restful sleep.

offerings of your
   choosing
scissors or prun-
   ing shears
basket
12 inches twine
nail or thumbtack

1. Invoke a sacred container around you and dedicate the container to whatever intention you have for your bundle. If you are making a seasonal blessing bundle, dedicate this sacred container to the sovereign magic of the season. Ask the Earth to offer leaves, branches, flowers, and other sacred items for your bundle.

2. When you are ready, begin your adventure out into the world. Allow your intention to lead the way. Place your offerings as you go and gather only that which is offered to you willingly and freely from the natural world. Snip your findings with your scissors or shears and carry them in your basket.

3. Once you have a good handful of natural material, return home. Trim the materials and bind them together with twine, tightly wrapping the base of the bundle and securing with a knot. You want the bundle to be secure but also loose.

continued >

Blessing Bundles *continued*

4. You can leave the bundle as is, bound at the base with the rest open like a bouquet, or you can use the rest of your twine to bind the other end.

5. With a small nail or thumbtack, hang the bundle above the inside of your front door.

6. When the next season arrives, burn the precious bundle. Save the ash to add to candles and sprinkle in your plants, on your altar, and with your offerings.

7. Replace with a new seasonal bundle at the beginning of each season.

Your House Altar

Your home is a temple and a living being. Remember that you don't live there alone—we all coexist with the spirits of the land, our ancestors, and guiding spirits. Creating a house altar to nourish your home is a wonderful way to continually honor all of its living gifts. This altar is the literal heart of your home. It channels source energy into your home, invokes your ancestral hearth, and filters out energy from the other altars and rooms within your dwelling. Here are some helpful tips for making your house altar.

- **Placement.** Choose a prominent location in the center of the home or wherever the altar can "see" as many rooms as possible. Witches often place their house altar in the living room.

- **Objects.** Choose a range of objects, tools, and offerings that call in groundedness, health, abundance, and ancestral spirit. For instance, on my house altar I have framed icons of Sara e Kali and the Czarna Madonna to honor my maternal and paternal ancestry. Along with fresh flowers and offerings, I also place a mirror on my altar to deflect any negative energy.

- **Hearth.** The hearth was the traditional central point of the home where we made food and medicine and gathered for warmth, stories, and community. Invoke its energy with a candle specifically blessed with the magic of the ancestral hearth

- **Nourishment.** The house altar is the most important altar to maintain for the sustained health of your home. As such, it needs consistent nourishment. Place a fresh glass of water on it daily, add fresh flowers and plants often, and serve a small portion of one of your meals to your altar at least once per week (leave overnight then compost).

Energy-Clearing Ritual for the Home

Our home is an extension of ourselves. What you're going through inside your own body, mind, and heart will echo throughout your home. This energy can be held by the walls, ceilings, and floors and if left untended has the potential to haunt you. The energy of our feelings can be held in the air, lingering in each room even well after the feelings have passed. This ritual will help lift any stagnant energy from your home. It's helpful to do this ritual after periods of sickness or depression, intense work weeks, or even disagreements with loved ones and housemates.

medium bowl
1 lemon
knife
paper and pen
matches or lighter
few drops lavender oil
fresh dill
black pepper

1. Invoke sacred space and arrange your ingredients on your altar.

2. Slice the lemon into thin rings and set aside.

3. On the piece of paper, write this invocation:

   Breath like dawn, inspire this home. Blood like gratitude, bring healing to this home. Bones like ceremony, bring stability to this home. Tears like remembering, bring wisdom to this home.

4. Visualize the energy you want to clear from your home. Have you been sick recently? Have you been struggling emotionally or financially? Have you had conflict in the home? Bring to mind the situation and invite resolution and the opening of new pathways forward.

5. When you're ready, burn your prayer in the bowl and allow it to turn to ash.

6. Next, fill the bowl with water. Cut the water with the knife by slicing from east to west,

then west to east, then north to south, and then south to north. This opens the water to receive your intentions.

7. Recite the spell while adding the slices of lemon, lavender oil, and herbs to the bowl.

8. Make one of these bowls for every room in your home and place a bowl somewhere prominent in each room. Leave for three nights.

9. On the morning of the fourth day, gather these bowls, ask the elements to transmute the energies into a healing salve for the spirits that tend to your home, and pour the contents of the bowls outside under your favorite tree or plant.

Mini Bathroom Rituals

Don't underestimate the power of the energy of your bathroom! The bathroom is where we are our most naked selves. For many of us, it's the place where we think, process feelings, and come to some of our most brilliant ideas and most challenging decisions. Here are a few ideas to keep the energy of your bathroom vibrant.

- **Ocean Filter.** During every Full Moon, place a glass of water containing 3 tablespoons of salt in each corner of your bathroom. Leave for three nights. These glasses conjure the vast capacity of the ocean to hold and heal, which is very helpful during times of deep emotional processing.

- **Higher Self Altar.** On your bathroom counter, make a small altar dedicated to your higher self. Place a small mirror faceup on your counter. Add a candle anointed with blessing oil and charged with affirming words. Light this candle when showering and getting ready in the bathroom. It will help you remember your true self, power, and resiliency.

- **Love Notes.** Never underestimate the immense power of small gestures, especially when centered in love. Leave yourself love notes on the bathroom mirror using either sticky notes or lipstick.

- **Customized Bath Products.** You can buy unscented body care products and add customized essential oil blends to them. Here is my go-to energy hygiene essential oil blend. Add it to unscented bath wash and enjoy.

- For every 4 ounces of body wash, add 2 drops of:

    - juniper (for purging energies and protection)
    - mugwort (for psychic cleansing and protection)
    - lavender (for psychic activation and connection to ancestors)
    - patchouli (for abundance and joy)

Houseplants as Helpers

My houseplants are my companions, confidants, roommates, advisors, and best friends! Plants hold a tremendous amount of space for their human counterparts and are witnesses to all that we are and all that we are experiencing. Like any good friend, our plants want to support us. Here is a sweet ritual to honor your plants' role in your life and nourish them in kind. This spell is inspired by my dear friend Kiki Robinson of The Opulent Witch.

pencil

1-by-1-inch piece of cotton fabric for each plant

small crystal

1. Invoke sacred space and center yourself. Sit with all your houseplants around you. Remember that your plants breathe. Slow your breath and try to connect to the breath of your plants. Reflect on all your plants do for your well-being and the mutual love you share.

2. One by one, ask each plant its name. Ask it what job or task it would like to have in the house. Does it want to work with energy—to help ground, protect, filter, and transmute the energy in the house? Or does it want to work with emotions—to help transmit, process, and ease emotions in the house?

3. Next, use your pencil to write the plant's name, its task, and a word of affirmation for its work on a square of fabric.

4. Hold the crystal and ask for its consent to work with the houseplant. Ask the crystal to be a trusted companion to your plant and help with its tasks.

continued >

5. Wrap the crystal in the cloth and push it into the soil of your plant's pot. Thank the plant and return it to its perch. Repeat for all your plants.

6. Remember to check in with your plants periodically and make any adjustments to your expectations as your plants and their crystal companion learn more about their tasks.

The Bedroom Portal

Your bedroom should be a sanctuary–the place where you can rest, unwind, and be yourself. This is a protection and boundary spell to keep your room free from your daily worries. It also serves as a receptacle to hold your thoughts and anxieties from the day so you don't bring them into your sanctuary. Reset this spell once a month by placing the braid outside at the Full Moon and returning it to your room the next evening.

1 red 13-foot long cord (about ¼ inch thick)

1 black 13-foot long cord (about ¼ inch thick)

1 white 13-foot long cord (about ¼ inch thick)

All-Purpose Ritual Oil (page 56)

1. Invoke sacred space and gather your ingredients.

2. Reflect on how you would like to feel in your bedroom. What kind of energy do you wish to invite in, and what kind do you wish to keep out?

3. With this in your mind, place a dime-sized amount of your ritual oil in your palm. Massage the oil into each of the cords, adding a dime-sized amount to your hands for each cord. As you massage the oil, envision the following for each cord:

   - **Black:** to protect against and banish unwanted energies

   - **White:** for healing and boundaries

   - **Red:** an invitation to your most sacred self

continued ›

4. Gather all three cords and tie them together at one end. Braid the cords together, envisioning their correspondences weaving into one powerful intention. Reflect on this braid as a protective threshold to your room.

5. When complete, tie a knot at the end of the braid. Hang it draped around your bedroom doorframe.

6. Conclude your ritual by releasing your sacred space.

Conclusion

By now, you've come far in your craft. Take a moment to reflect on all the work you've done. You have an understanding of the foundational principles of traditional magic and practical witchcraft, are armed with basic tools and spell crafting techniques, and have practiced spells and rituals for your health, relationships, and home. You've also been tracking your progress and honoring your learning by updating your grimoire and personalizing your rituals. Now that we've laid some pretty solid foundations, let's move onto more dynamic ritual.

7

CAREER, SUCCESS, AND PROSPERITY

I love the deep feeling of satisfaction I get from working and earning money. Work can bring great purpose to our lives. Money is also important, of course, but we shouldn't define our worth by how much we have. When identifying what a successful and prosperous life means for you, consider your wellness, relationships, passions, and joys. Abundance takes many forms. You can value money but understand that it is not the whole picture. This chapter presents rituals and spells to help you redefine your relationship with success, prosperity, and abundance to better align with your values.

Get Clear on Your Values and Goals

I find that defining my values is very helpful when working toward my goals. Many of us spend tons of time and effort pursuing academic, career, and relationship goals only to realize later that we were chasing the dreams of other people. Or maybe at some point, you silenced your passions out of fear of what others would think or because your passions felt overwhelming, confusing, or trivial. Sometimes we just don't have clarity on where we want to apply our energy. Or maybe you've accomplished a pretty major goal or had a major life shift . . . and aren't sure what to do next. Taking a values inventory is a great and necessary step in refocusing and preparing for your personal and professional goals. You'll find an Abundance Values Inventory on page 135.

As you connect with your values, you also want to define what success and abundance mean to you. They mean different things for everyone! For me, a successful life is one rich in resources to share and meet the needs of self and community without strain, struggle, or worry. An abundant life is one that gives me strength to lift my head and continue forward while deepening my connection to spirit.

Before you start the rituals and spells in this chapter, take 10 minutes to write and sketch in your grimoire about what success and abundance mean to you personally.

IDENTIFY BARRIERS

There are many hidden barriers to achieving your goals, one of the biggest being false belief systems and internalization of systemic oppression. At times it might be necessary to cut cords with false beliefs like self-doubt or not being worthy of success. You may also want to examine your relationship to any cultural and social privileges you benefit from and how those inform your goals and how you approach them. If you don't take time to understand the inherent privileges or very real barriers that exist due to how people are politicized and leveraged against each other, you may be convinced that the ease with which you manifest is directly correlated with the strength of your magic rather than your privilege. Before attempting any spell, take time to clarify your intention and examine any underlying belief systems that might distract you or steal you away from your values. This way you can address and account for any barriers to your work in advance.

Spells and Rituals for Professional and Creative Success

In the following you will find an assortment of spells, meditations, and preparations to help you focus your magic toward achieving your goals. Feel free to modify and riff off them as you desire. Don't forget to track your learning and your progress in your journal as you go along. This learned wisdom is essential as you build your magical practice and even more crucial when working magic for success and abundance!

Abundance Anointing Oil

This oil is perfect for attracting success to you. Anoint your body with the oil before a big interview or while working on an important project. Anoint your money with it to spread wealth and ensure that what you spend generates abundant energy back to you. Add it to candles and spells to jump-start your luck. Begin this oil at the New Moon and let it cure until the next New Moon. No need to strain.

Remember, New Moon to Full Moon is the time to increase and gather energy; Full Moon to New Moon is for releasing and clearing.

fireproof bowl

your tarot deck

green votive candle

matches or lighter

4 bay leaves

glass jar with lid

pen and paper

piece of paper currency

bottle of olive oil

offerings: an apple,
   spare change

1. Set the fireproof bowl in front of you and place the ingredients and offerings around it.

2. Pull the Wheel of Fortune card from your tarot deck and place it under the bowl.

3. Recite the following enchantment

   Air above, Earth below, Fire within, Water around. With gratitude, I call the elements to this altar. Clear and open the paths of blessing before, within, behind, and all around me. Devour any obstacles to my success and transform their energy into blessings of abundance with ease and grace. So it is.

4. Light the candle. Envision each element blessing the bay leaves, one by one, with increasing abundance. Once your leaves are charged, place them in your jar.

5. Reflect on what true abundance means to you (finance, relationship, health, creativity, etc.). Write these reflections on the paper and then burn it in the bowl. Add the ash to the jar.

6. Add the currency and then the olive oil to the jar. Put the lid on the jar and shake while reciting the preceding enchantment. Place the jar in the bowl.

7. Let the candle burn down. Close your ritual space, and gift your offerings.

Self-Worth Spell

Our belief in self can make a big difference in how we approach circumstances and goals. Our relationship with self is a constant work in progress. We don't need to "arrive" to a complete version of ourselves in order to experience joy, success, love, or happiness. It is all about the journey. It is important, however, to have compassion and love for ourselves as we learn, change, grow, and achieve. This spell is helpful to cast when you experience feelings of self-doubt that diminish your self-worth. Feel free to modify this spell to tend to any quality of personal power that needs a boost.

photo of yourself
pen
pink pillar candle
  and holder
St. John's wort oil
silver coin
12 white roses
rhodochrosite

1. Set your sacred space and reflect on your self-worth. On the back of your photo, write words affirming your worth, confidence, brilliance, power, and anything else to bolster your sense of worth.

2. Using the pen, carve a pentagram into the pillar candle, envisioning all the elements coming together to empower your sense of self-worth and clear the energies inhibiting you. You can also carve in the words you wrote on the back of your photo as well as any additional empowering symbols.

3. Anoint the candle with the St. John's wort oil, envisioning the candle as an extension of yourself. As the oil fills and smooths the carvings, imagine it removing your self-doubt and making room for your worth to bloom.

4. Arrange your altar. Place your picture in the middle and place the silver coin and the rhodochrosite on the picture. Place the candle above your photo and place the white roses in a complete circle around the altar.

5. Light the candle and speak the words of affirmation you wrote on your picture and inscribed into the candle. Allow the candle to burn, extinguishing it and relighting it as needed until it is completely burned down.

6. Place the image on your bathroom mirror and carry your rhodochrosite daily to remind you of your power and worth. Bury your silver coin in your favorite place in nature as an offering.

7. Hang the roses to dry. Add the dried petals to baths and incense whenever you need an extra boost of self-confidence.

Job-Hunting Charm

This is a simple charm to use when job hunting or applying for a new gig. You can use this charm to enchant your résumés and job applications and charge a talisman. A witch once told me to add this phrase to the end of any procurement spell: "Grant me this or something better," so I recommend doing that here! You can adapt this charm for admissions applications as well, including for grants, training programs, school programs, and residencies.

paper and pen
talisman to charge
  (such as an acorn,
  quartz crystal, or
  found pebble)
copy of your résumé
  or application (either
  digital or hard copy)
Abundance Anointing
  Oil (see page 130)

1. At the beginning of your job search, make a list of the things you wish to learn, goals you want to accomplish, and everything you are looking for with this new job, position, or placement.

2. When your list feels complete, anoint your hands and your talisman of choice with your anointing oil while reciting this charm nine times:

   My magic now I liberate with each choice
   I make. With every step, first one then two, and
   three by three, I call abundance now to me. My
   mind, my path, my heart be clear.
   I call good work and wisdom here.

3. Next, hold your talisman in your hands and recite the preceding charm at least nine times while visualizing all the desires you listed out from your earlier reflection. Then begin your search and filling out your applications.

4. Place your charged talisman on your completed résumé, application, computer, and phone before submitting them.

5. Recite this charm and carry your talisman as you go job hunting, go out for interviews, or submit your résumé or application.

Abundance Values Inventory

Before working toward a goal, it's important to take time to understand your personal values around abundance. We can make more informed choices when our values and goals are aligned. Revisit this inventory often as you make progress on your goals to ensure that you are still aligning with your abundance values. If not, perhaps you need to redirect your goal or update one of your values. The inventory is a work in progress, meant to be repeated as you set and achieve new goals throughout your life.

your journal and pen

cup of your favorite tea

1. Reflect on each of the following prompts and spend a few minutes writing your responses in your journal:

   How do you define abundance?

   What is your experience with receiving abundance in its various forms (financial, relational, etc.)?

   What is your experience with giving abundance in its various forms?

   Do you believe that your productivity is a direct indication of your worth?

   How would your relationship with abundance change if you didn't place your worth on your productivity?

2. From your written reflections, generate a list of six specific principles that define your relationship with abundance. These principles will act as your abundance value system, guiding your choices and behavior as you chase your goals. As an example, here is a recent Abundance Values Inventory I completed:

continued >

Abundance Values Inventory *continued*

a. I will fight for indigenous communities and black American descendants of African peoples sold into slavery.

b. I prioritize mutual care in all of my personal and professional choices.

c. I value accessibility to resources and wealth redistribution.

d. I know that my self-worth is not dependent upon my productivity.

e. My choices to survive and thrive are not acts of desperation.

f. The financial choices I make today will set me up for success in the future.

Good Luck Bundle

This is a good luck charm for you to carry throughout each day to attract the subtle grace of abundance. Carry this bundle in your pocket, wallet, or bag. You can recharge the bundle by anointing it with your Abundance Anointing Oil (page 130) and leaving it on your altar from the Balsamic Moon through the New Moon and then using again after the Crescent Moon.

7-by-7-inch square of yellow, gold, or green fabric

piece of paper currency

pen

Abundance Anointing Oil (page 130)

3 pieces of copper or pyrite or 3 pennies

3 apple seeds and remaining apple (as an offering to the spirits)

piece of jewelry that you wish to repurpose

extra ingredient that represents good luck to you

12 inches red string

1. Set your container and arrange your materials into an altar with your square of cloth in the center.

2. On the piece of paper currency, cross out the treasury secretary's name and write in your name. Inscribe symbols and words to affirm your luck and abundance on both sides of this bill. Anoint it with a few drops of your Abundance Anointing Oil.

3. Next, anoint the 3 copper pieces, pennies, or pyrite with oil and envision blessings and luck coming your way. Wrap the objects in the paper currency.

4. Place the currency bundle in the center of your fabric square.

5. With a few drops of oil, anoint the 3 apple seeds. Hold them in your hand and ask them to help you grow your luck and abundance. Place the seeds in a triangle around the currency bundle.

continued ➤

Good Luck Bundle *continued*

6. Anoint the piece of reclaimed jewelry. Charge it with the blessing of your ancestors and guiding spirits. Envision infinite grace supporting all of your endeavors. Place the jewelry on top of your currency bundle.

7. Hold your secret ingredient, asking it to bring a strong and healthy relationship with luck and abundance into your life. Add it to the fabric square.

8. Complete your bundle by folding the edges of the fabric square around all of your ingredients, making sure everything is held securely. Wrap the string tightly around the bundle and tie with a knot.

9. Release your container and offer your apple to the elemental spirits outside. Take your bundle with you whenever you need an extra dose of abundance.

Meditation to Bolster Success

The mind is the witch's most powerful ritual tool. Repeating an active meditation or visualization can powerfully shift our focus. When a visualization is imbued with magical energy, it can be channeled into actions to effect real change in the world. As with other active meditations, feel free to modify the content to suit your personal preferences.

soothing music
  (optional)
altar candle
matches or lighter
dried rosemary
fireproof bowl
your journal

1. Set your container and find a comfortable seated position. If you would like to use soothing music to support your meditation, begin playing that music in the background.

2. Light your candle. Set an intention for its flame to gently transmute blockages into openings for blessings. Place a small amount of rosemary in your fireproof bowl and light it for protection and clarity.

3. Turn your awareness inward and slowly direct it toward your inner success altar.

4. Begin to make your way to that altar. Allow yourself to observe the path laid out before you. What do you notice there? Are there any obstacles preventing you from moving forward? Concentrate only on the path. Do not veer from the path or seek obstacles off the path.

5. Imagine that you have an implement you can use to clear these obstacles. Visualize that you also have a receptacle to carry them in after you have cleared them from the path.

continued >

6. Continue to make your way to your altar of success, clearing any obstacles that are blocking your path. If you find objects that you can step over or maneuver around, leave them.

7. Once you arrive at your altar, envision a cauldron that contains an eternal flame of abundance. Feel the power of this fire. When you are ready, begin to feed this fire with the obstacles you've collected and cleared from your path. Add them one by one, allowing them each to catch fire and slowly burn. Receive the energy of abundance each object releases as it burns. What beliefs are being reshaped as these obstacles burn?

8. When you're done with this, allow the fire to settle back down into the cauldron. Thank your altar and return back down the path until you return to the present moment.

9. Repeat this meditation as often as you need until the path to your altar of success remains clear. This exercise will help you keep the path forward in your daily life clear and obstacle-free.

10. Close your container. Make notes about your experience in your journal.

Get Paid Candle Spell

This simple spell goes a long way when you are due for a promotion, are about to ask for that raise, need to call in a favor, or have to ask someone to settle up a debt. As with any procurement or petitionary spell, you will need to accompany it with actionable steps toward your intent. Remember, the simplest spells require the deepest relationships with the ingredients and your intent. Before casting, reflect on your Abundance Values Inventory (page 135) and make any needed revisions.

1 oak leaf or bay leaf

pen

seven-day candle in the color that best corresponds to your abundance values

9 coins (preferably copper pennies)

Abundance Anointing Oil (page 130)

1 piece of paper currency

few strands of your hair, saliva, or nail clippings

fireproof bowl

matches or lighter

1. Set your sacred space and arrange your items on your altar.

2. Reflect on your intended outcome of your spell. Clarify your intention and write it on the oak or bay leaf. (You can use multiple leaves if you need more space.)

3. Place the candle in the middle of the altar and arrange the 9 coins in a circle around the candle. These coins represent the resources around you and define a clear and protected path for blessings to arrive and be received by you.

4. For this spell, simpler is better. Don't get too fancy, too wordy, or too mired in compli-cated recipes. You can use your Abundance Anointing Oil to anoint the pennies, the leaves, and your candle. Repeat your intent with each step.

5. Cross out the name of the treasury secre-tary on the currency and add your name there instead. Draw empowering symbols of prosperity and affirming words all over the bill. Include the dollar amount you desire

continued >>

from this promotion, raise, or conversation. Keep in mind that spells depend greatly on your relationship with intent and ingredients. This number needs to be reasonable and achievable. You can always modify this spell for a higher amount as your circumstances and relationship with financial prosperity change.

6. Add your hair, nail clippings, or a little saliva to the center of the bill. Fold up the bill and place it in front of your candle inside of the circle of coins.

7. Place your leaf in the fireproof bowl and burn it. Add the ash from the burnt leaves to your candle. Repeat your intention and light the candle.

8. Allow the candle to burn, releasing your intention into the world and blessing the coins and your bundle.

9. When the candle has burned down, place the bundle in your wallet. Carry it with you for sustained prosperity. Gather the coins and carry them with you, gifting one to the world over the next 9 days as an act of gratitude.

Windfall Spell

We all have moments in life when cash is tight. Emergencies happen, and we can't always avoid surprise expenses. This spell is ideally practiced as soon as you know a windfall is needed. It can help recapitulate the energy of anxiety and fear that comes with financial stress into a magnet for swift financial gain. A note of caution: Please be sure to include a prayer for ease, grace, health, and wellness for yourself and everyone you know and love. This precaution will help prevent cash coming to you via devastation or personal harm. When it comes to the offerings in this spell, be as generous as you can. Think lovely flowers, whiskey, apples, organ meats, and other delights. When cash is tight, buying these things can be challenging; you can always simply offer what you have.

generous offering to the elemental spirits
pen
5 votive candles in holders
blank check
tarot deck

1. Set your sacred container. This spell is also an altar, and you will be casting your spell as you build your altar.

2. Using your pen, inscribe the amount of windfall you need on each of the candles.

3. Next write your blank check out to yourself in the amount of the windfall that you need. Sign the check in the name of the Universe. Place it in the center of your altar with the Wheel of Fortune card underneath and the Sun card on top.

4. Around the check, place the Ace cards on your altar in the direction of their corresponding elements: east (Air), south (Fire), west (Water), north (Earth). As you do, envision the elements infusing your spell and altar with steadily increasing yet non-destructive energy—a gentle spark that grows into a nourishing hearth flame, not a raging forest fire.

continued >

5. Place a candle on top of each card, starting with the center. Summon the catalytic power of the elements and invite them to answer your request with swift ease and integrative grace. Feel free to select candle colors that correspond to the elements: Air (yellow), Fire (red), Water (blue), Earth (green), Center/Spirit (white).

6. Finally, place your offerings at the center of your altar around the middle candle. Invite the elements and Source to be nourished by this offering.

7. Once the candles completely burn down, gather the offerings, take them outside, and bury them someplace lovely. Keep the cards on your altar and feed the spell with new candles for the next 7 days.

A Sigil for Successful Completion of Goals

Sigils are a powerful and relatively simple form of magic suitable for nearly every circumstance, especially when we want to sustain an intention over time. Sigils are most powerful when they are crafted from symbols that have personal significance and are designed around specific intentions. The magic of sigils comes from the power the witch assigns to each symbol they weave into its design. In chapter 5, we used empowered words to create a sigil to serve as a protective ward for our home. For this spell, we will be working with symbols rather than words. You can craft a new sigil to focus your energy and intention for each new goal you chase.

pen and paper

anything you need to aid your focus, such as a candle or a cup of tea

1. Define the goal you are working on, listing out the major and necessary steps required to successfully accomplish this goal.

2. Reflect on any obvious barriers to your completion of this goal.

3. List a word to embody each step of your process.

4. List a word to embody any barrier to your success.

5. Reflect on the list embodying the steps to your process and let your imagination find a shape that represents the list as a whole. I suggest sticking to basic shapes like a star, triangle, circle, square, arc, or spiral. Doodle the shapes that come to you while you reflect on this list until you begin to resonate with one or two of them. If you resonate with more than one, begin to

continued >

combine the shapes you feel connected to until they form a single shape that embodies your list of steps.

6. Next, reflect on the list of potential barriers. Repeat the process in step 5, except envision and doodle shapes that represent these barriers having been transformed into energy of opportunity and resources.

7. Combine the two symbols to form the sigil that represents the successful completion of your goal. Draw this sigil on a new piece of paper.

8. Place the sigil on your altar, commit it to memory, and meditate on this sigil while working toward your goal. I find that when I'm stuck, drawing this sigil and tracing its lines generates momentum.

9. When the goal is complete, burn your sigil to release the energy to make room for the next endeavor.

Protection Ritual for Those Who Hustle

This is an invocation to summon protection for those who run multiple hustles and work multiple gigs to make ends meet. It can be exhausting to have to recalibrate from one job to the next. Perform this protective ritual before you begin your workday and repeat as needed throughout the day.

1. Find a comfortable seated position. Take a few moments to center yourself at your inner altar.

2. Bring your attention to your breath. On each inhalation, summon the four elements to you. With each exhalation, release all doubt and uncertainty to the elements to transmute. Repeat for seven breaths.

3. Continue to breathe naturally. Now, visualize the elements one by one in sync with your breath:

    * **Air:** Imagine a gentle breeze moving from the east and circling all around you. Notice the qualities of the air on your skin.

    * **Fire:** Imagine a gentle fire, warm and protective, encircling you. See it dancing with Air and weaving a sphere of protection all around you.

    * **Water:** Imagine a cool and restorative stream flowing around you. Observe it as it weaves together with the sphere of the Air and the Fire.

    * **Earth:** Imagine a grounding force strengthening your boundaries as it integrates itself into this elemental sphere.

4. One by one release the living elements, asking them to seal your sphere.

5. Spend a few minutes exploring this sphere of protection around you. What do you notice? What do you feel?

6. When you finish your day, reverse this meditation to release this sphere.

Conclusion

Now that you've worked these rituals, how do you determine success? What is a prosperous life? How do you define abundance? Are your answers different than they were at the beginning of this chapter? What's come up for you around the concepts of wealth, money, success, and abundance? If you've experienced a shift in priorities, think about which rituals you need to perform to support and empower this shift. Write your new rituals and track any impact these shifts have on your relationships, abundance, and your personal values. Now that you've worked your craft to support the major areas of life, let's explore how to apply it to your day-to-day circumstances.

SIMPLE WITCHCRAFT FOR THE EVERYDAY

I n our day-to-day lives, so many things happen that are out of our control and with no good or clear reason. Luckily, we can draw on our craft to respond in an empowered way when things catch us off guard. Magic is a practice. Practice doesn't make perfect—but it does make us prepared. This chapter offers spells and rituals to help you apply your magic to the myriad situations, experiences, and challenges that pop up in daily life.

Spells and Rituals for Daily Life

Here is a collection of meditations, rituals, charms, and recommendations to integrate your craft into your daily life. I've also included sections with helpful tips for better sleep and how to work with offerings to deepen your connection to the spirits of nature.

Before diving in, make a list of some recent circumstances that have surprised you. Reflect on the work you've done so far and try writing a few rituals that might help you navigate these situations. Draw upon the wisdom you've cultivated from your lived experiences and the magical knowledge you've gained from your practice. The practical application of magic requires an unwavering faith in self and a deep trust in what you know to be true. Trust yourself to be supported. Make magic happen daily.

Harnessing
Environmental Essences

We can harness the essence of our environment and the seasons as a way to imbue ourselves with the magic of the moment—aligning ourselves to the power of time and place and syncing our altars with that of the world around us. You can harness the essence of astrological alignments, weather manifestations, times of day, plants, and place by building an altar to represent those forces, gathering a bowl of water on that altar, and blessing it with your intentions through the lens of those forces. Before performing this spell, sit with the environment you wish to make an essence from and ask for permission. You can do this by making offerings to the spirits that tend to that place, asking permission, and clearly communicating your intentions. This can take a few visits; it takes time to establish a safe and trusting relationship.

offerings to the spirits
altar to embody that
which you are making
an essence from
large glass bowl
large jar of distilled water

1. Go to where you wish to make your essence and gift your offerings, ask permission, and restate your intentions.

2. Set your container and build your altar. Place your glass bowl in the center of the altar.

   a. If you are making an environmental altar, center your altar in the landscape. If you are gathering the essence of a plant, center it as near the plant as possible without disturbing it. For seasonal, elemental, or weather essences center the altar and bowl in a clearing. For celestial and astrological essences build the altar at the time of the transits you are wishing to harness.

3. Fill the large bowl with blessed water and repeat your intentions.

continued >

4. Meditate in that place while your altar gathers the essence being shared with you. Leave your altar and bowl of water to gather the essence for at least one hour and up to 24 hours.

5. Pour the water back into the jar and seal it. You can also create a sigil to embody the essence and draw that sigil on the lid of the jar.

6. Release your sacred space, gather your altar and return home.

7. You can bath in this water, feed your plants with it, or use it in other rituals.

8. If you wish to ingest this water you will need to preserve it with 1 part original water to 2 parts grain alcohol or vegetable glycerin.

Healing Ritual for Your Houseplants

I love houseplants. I am the proud parent of 46 houseplants–and I'm not shy to admit that I love them more than most people! If you have houseplants, you know how devastating it is when they start to look sick, especially if you've been tending to them with the right nutrients, soil, light, temperature, and water conditions. Here is a simple healing ritual for sick plants.

1 quartz crystal point
(small enough to fit in
the spray bottle)
bowl of water
spray bottle

1. Invoke sacred space, calling to the healing energies of the elements.

2. Communicate with your plants. Ask them to share with you what is going on for them and how they are feeling.

3. Hold your quartz point and ask it to hold the healing energies of the elements. Invite the elements to imbue this quartz point with their healing energy. Place the quartz in the bowl of water.

4. Connecting to your inner altar (see page 62), call the healing energies of the elements to you and envision this energy pooling around your hands. Place your hands in the water and invite the healing energies to pass from your hands and be held by the water.

5. Pour the water and quartz into the spray bottle. Spray the leaves and soil of your houseplants gently every few days.

6. Repeat as needed until your plants begin to recover.

continued ›

7. A few tips for maintenance:

   a. Bless your plants every time you feed and water them, asking the sun, soil, water, and air to nourish them.

   b. Spend a few intentional breaths with each of your plants each day.

   c. Connect with your plants every morning and evening. Lay hands on them and greet them with kind thoughts and communication.

Blessing for Animal Companions

The only being I love more than my plants is my dog. She is the light of my life and my most treasured mirror. If you have the joy and honor of taking care of an animal companion, you know the unique magic they bring. Their happiness and wellness are our responsibility. They sacrifice so much to teach us and tend to us. Here is a practical blessing you can offer them anytime. You may also modify almost every spell from chapters four and six to focus on the magical care of your animal companion.

1. Invoke sacred space and connect to your inner altar (see page 62). Imagine the love you and your animal companion share at the center of that altar.

2. Call the power of the elements to further imbue this love with their magic. Allow this fortified love to expand until it fills you up.

3. With your breath, direct this energy into your hands. With each inhale, envision this energy pooling into your palms. With every exhale, allow it to emanate outward from your hands.

4. Next, offer a healing and protective touch to your animal companion. Many of our animal companions enjoy being near us and held by us. Use this closeness as an opportunity to transmit this energy of fortified love emanating from your inner altar through your hands.

5. When complete, release the elements from your inner altar. Direct the remaining energies outward from your inner altar, out through your hands, and into the space around you so it fills the rooms of your home.

6. Release this sacred space. Repeat this ritual as often as desired.

Note: If your animal companion doesn't enjoy touch or it is unsafe for them to be touched, simply transmit this energy through meditation.

Spell to Console a Friend

This simple spell will bless an amulet of comfort and protection to console a friend in need. The beauty of an amulet, charm, or talisman is that they do not need to be relationally dependent to work and they can be released at any point; destroy the amulet to break the spell. Remember that it's important to get consent before blessing another person. This also gives your friend an opportunity to tell you exactly how they wish to be supported. Sometimes simply knowing that someone has our back is all we need.

1 small pebble, lovingly selected while thinking of your friend

single rose in any color

13 inches white string

4-by-4-inch square of blue fabric

1. Center yourself and invoke the love you have for your friend. Hold the pebble in your hand. Continue to invoke this love and massage it into the pebble until it warms.

2. Place the pebble into the heart of the rose. Envision the pebble grounding your friend. Watch them find stability in the love and support that surround them. Imagine the rose holding them and softening the impact of whatever it is that they are going through.

3. Take the white string and summon healing and protective energies. Tightly wrap the rose blossom with the string in order to secure the pebble inside. Tie the string tightly at the base of the bloom and clip the stem at least 3 inches from the knot.

4. Wrap the amulet in the blue cloth and tie the fabric with the remaining white string.

5. Give the amulet to your friend and have them hang it in the window of their bedroom until the rose is dry. Once it's dry, they should carry it around with them or leave it in their room.

6. Once the hardship has passed, tell them to burn the bundle and bathe in its ashes.

7. They should continue to carry the pebble as a grounding stone or return it to the Earth in gratitude.

Rituals for Better Sleep and Vivid Dreams

Sleep is a sacred time. Physiologically, it's when our body restores itself from the stress of the day. I also believe that our spiritual vitality, psychic energy, and minds are restored during sleep. If you find that your sleep is being disturbed because of stressful circumstances or emotional pain, magic can help ease some of this disruption. The following tips will help give you access to deeper states of rest and restoration during sleep.

- **Build a Dream Altar.** Remember that altars are external representations of our internal wishes, desires, and circumstances. Build a dream altar by placing items that represent calm, protection, deep sleep, healing, and restoration by or under your bed. Each night before bed, spend 10 to 15 minutes with this altar reflecting on your day. Allow this altar to hold your thoughts and concerns while you sleep so you have more room for rest and dreaming.

- **Set a Sacred Container for Sleep.** Sleep, like any ritual, is best performed in a sacred and intentional space. Before bed, set a container by saying a prayer of protection, rest, and deep restorative sleep.

- **Change Your Sheets.** It is important that to treat our bed like a shrine. Bedsheets are altar cloths that hold us and tend to us while we sleep. At least once a week, take your sheets off, air them out, launder them, and apply the following clearing spray to your mattress before remaking your bed.

- **Clearing Spray for Sleep.** To promote sleep and rest, add 4 drops of the following essential oils to every 4 ounces of distilled water. Use as desired.

  - Lavender
  - Chamomile
  - Petitgrain
  - Clary sage

Magic to Bless, Protect, and Cleanse Your Home

One of the most effective ways to transmute energy, purge obstacles, and clear the path before you is to use effigies, burn bundles, and poppets. These are old forms of magic that have survived through countless generations. This means they hold an intrinsic power that is activated inside the witch when we use them in our magical workings. Along with candle spells, burn bundles, poppets, and effigies can serve a wide range of purposes, especially around healing and transformation.

- **Bundles.** Bundles draw upon the innate magic of the ingredients used to channel direct energy around a situation. I make bundles out of dried altar flowers, written prayers bound up with string, or seasonal foliage to harness the raw power of the living elements. These are great for fast spells on the fly or to use as charms to diffuse a particular energy in a space over a longer period of time.

- **Effigies.** Effigies are objects or sculptures made to represent ancestors or spirits you wish to petition. They serve as a body through which those beings can emanate their magic into your home. They can also represent particular people, unwanted energies, or circumstances that you wish to banish. As you craft the effigy, you will want to hold your intentions very clearly in your mind and heart. To conclude your work with an effigy, it is traditional to burn it.

- **Poppets.** Poppets function similarly to effigies except that they serve as a surrogate self for the person they represent. This means you can enact your intentions upon a poppet to affect the person it represents. Poppets are traditionally made of braided rags or a sewn doll and often contain small bundles stuffed with written prayers, herbs, oils, or other ingredients that embody the intentions of the poppet. They are best burned by the person they represent or the witch who created them once they fulfill their purpose.

For Difficult Choices

Life is full of choices, many of which are challenging. To say yes to one thing requires saying no to another. And what happens when you change your mind? How do you redirect? Whether you have already made a decision and are realizing you actually need to change your course of action or you are simply faced with a significant choice, this spell will help guide your path.

your tarot deck
paper and pen
3 or 4 white votive
  candles
fireproof bowl
matches or lighter

1. Set your altar and pull the following cards out of your deck: the two of swords, the queen of swords, the chariot, and the moon.

2. On separate pieces of paper, write each choice you're facing. Then list the pros and cons of each choice. Try to narrow them down to two options if possible. If you end up with three choices, you need an extra candle to represent that choice.

3. Charge one candle for each option. Fold your pro and con lists for each choice and place them on your altar. Set the corresponding candle on top of each list.

4. Next take the remaining candle and charge it with the energy of your higher self, reflecting on your ability to make good choices at this time. Trust that you have all the information and resources you need. Trust that when you make the decision to move forward in a particular direction, additional resources will reveal themselves to you. Place that final candle in the center of your altar and arrange all the other candles around that candle.

5. Place the two of swords faceup between where you sit and the candles. Place the chariot, the queen of swords, and the moon card facedown in a line between the two of cups and the candles.

6. Light the candles and let them burn down completely, clearing the way for the best choice to emerge.

7. Once the candles burn, feel the choice that you are called to make become clear. Reflect on the clarity of your choice. Take the list of pros and cons related to that choice and place it in the center of your altar. Clear everything from your altar except the tarot cards and your list. Turn all the cards over.

8. Place the moon card in the center of your altar. Take the folded list of your choice and place it on the moon card. Then take the chariot card and place it facedown on top of both the moon card and the list. Next take the queen of swords and place it faceup on top of that stack. Place the two of swords card facedown beneath the stack of cards. Allow these to rest on your altar for the next 3 days while you affirm your choice.

9. When the 3 days are up, commit to your decision and take the action steps required to devote yourself to that choice resolutely.

10. Burn your list in your fireproof bowl, and bathe in the ashes.

Ease for Traveling

I love to travel, but it can also cause me a lot of anxiety–about traffic, delays, waiting in lines, and other snafus. As a transgender person, I also experience anxiety about the very invasive screening process required at airport security. Here is a simple spell to clear potential obstacles from your travel plans and ensure that you arrive to your destination safely and on time–and with limited anxiety.

shoelace

1. Before you set out on your adventure, take a few moments to breathe the prayer found in the Daily Protection Ritual (see page 52), modifying it to suit your travel plans. When you feel safe and contained in that prayer of protection, visualize any obstacle or challenge being gently and completely cleared away out of your travel path.

2. Repeat this visualization over and over and over again. When you are content in the knowledge and belief that all obstacles to your travel have been easily removed, grab your shoestring.

3. Tie a knot in the center of the string. Imagine any potential obstacle or challenge being bound within that knot. Take a few breaths and concentrate all of those obstacles into that knot.

4. Take three more breaths and begin untying the knot. As you do so, imagine that you are unfolding the obstacles and releasing them, making the path before you clear.

5. Then reconnect to that sphere of protection around you and begin your journey. You can hang the shoestring over your rearview mirror if traveling by car or tuck it into your pocket or luggage to carry it with you and keep your path forward clear.

Oil for Emotional Boundaries

We all respond to emotional energy in our own unique ways. Some of us recoil, some of us project our feelings onto others, and some of us might even neglect our own emotional state to prioritize the caretaking of others. There are lots of reasons for these differences, including conditioning, trauma, and learned defensive behaviors. Wherever we fall on the spectrum, it's important to identify our boundaries so we do not get sucked into the emotional energy of others. This oil will help you maintain your boundaries, reminding you what is and isn't yours to carry. I suggest making a large batch and dividing it into smaller bottles you can take with you and grab when the situation calls for it.

pen

1 bay leaf

fireproof bowl

matches or lighter

1 teaspoon of sea salt

juniper, mugwort, and rosemary essential oils (or 1 teaspoon of each dried herb)

16-ounce bottle of olive oil

7 thorns (from any thorny plant such as a rose, cactus, or blackberry)

1. Envision a pentagram and the way it represents the unity of all elements and empowers the magic of a witch's altar. Using your pen, draw that pentagram on the bay leaf, infusing it with the power of protection and resources of the elements.

2. In the fireproof bowl, light the bay leaf and let it burn to ash.

3. Add the salt and ash to the bottle of olive oil.

4. Next, add 9 drops of the juniper, mugwort, and rosemary essentials oils to the bottle of olive oil. (If you are using dried herbs, add 1 teaspoon of each to the olive oil.)

5. Now hold the thorns in your hand and imagine that they emanate a shield of protection that reinforces your emotional boundaries. When you sense that you are connected to the shield of the thorns, add them to the bottle of olive oil.

6. Feel free to add any other protective ingredients to the bottle. If you plan to share this oil

with others, avoid including any personal ingredients such as a strand of your hair.

7. Place the top on the bottle and shake it to mix the ingredients and fuse the oil with your boundaries. Place it on your altar and let it cure for at least 3 days.

8. Use the oil to anoint your body every day in the mornings and before bed. I like to place the oil on my heart, throat, hands, and feet and a little to the top of my head. You can also mix the oil into your everyday lotion and apply it to your entire body this way.

9. You may want to pour some into a small bottle to carry around with you every day to empower your boundaries. You can also give a small bottle to someone who might be having a hard day.

Daily Offerings

Sometimes we don't know what kind of ritual or spell to do about a particular experience. When in doubt, make offerings to the guiding spirits, elements, and ancestors. Even if you don't know it, these beings are vigilantly watching out for you. Offerings are personal, nourishing, nurturing, supportive, and so easy to do. Sometimes all the magic needed is tending to the relationships that will see us through our struggles. Here are some considerations.

- **What to Offer.** Every spirit you're in a relationship with will have their own preferences for offerings. Until you know these preferences, it's okay to simply gift them things that feel nourishing to you. You and the spirit can negotiate these offerings as you build your relationship. If you are pledging devotion to a particular spirit, you will want to know and learn what they prefer as offerings in order to give those offerings properly.

- **Where to Place Them.** Placement of your offerings depends greatly on the nature of your relationship with the spirits you're working with. For instance, when I'm building a relationship with the spirits of land, I will take offerings to a place in nature, outside my home, or in my yard. I also like to leave offerings to particular spirits on my house altar (see page 117) and the individual altars that are devoted to them.

- **How to Dispose of Them.** I leave flowers until they begin to wilt, and then I bundle and dry them for use in later spell crafting. For food items, I wait until they begin to turn and decompose before I compost them or carry them to a place in nature. If they are beverages like water or spirits, I wait until the liquid begins to evaporate from the glass and then pour the remaining libations on the ground outside my home. Never flush offerings of abundance or petition down the toilet or drain!

Make Offerings Daily. Whether in the form of incense, a thoughtful hello or greeting to your altars, or a glass of fresh water, it is important to share gratitude with your altars and spirits every day. These are relationships that you are tending. If you tend well to them, you will be supported in your intentions and spell crafting. No one ever likes to be that friend who people only call when they need something or want something! Your spirit guides feel the same way. I also like to carry a bag of blended herbs and biodegradable offerings and leave little gifts as I move through the world.

Conclusion

In this chapter, we wove various aspects from earlier spells, rituals, and exercises together to build rituals to meet the specific needs of unique situations. As we conclude our journey together, think about what you are taking away from the experience of exploring this grimoire. How will you integrate these learnings into your personal practice? Magic is flexible, offering the witch a cunning adaptability that can be leveraged in navigating almost any circumstance with purpose and meaning. Spend some time making a list of the circumstances you are currently facing. Are there spells in this grimoire to help you address these circumstances? If you haven't found a spell to address your specific situation, how can you take the structures of the spells in this grimoire and craft your own unique rituals? Magic is a practice, and the work of the witch is a craft; your learning is lifelong. Return to the basics as often as you need, cross-reference your ingredients, and double-check your resources. I can't wait for you to discover what you're capable of.

A Final Note

You've reached the end of this book, but you are only at the beginning of your witch's path. I hope the lessons, spells, and rituals here provide a strong foundation for the next chapter in your magical walk. Where will you go now? That depends entirely on what you have learned about yourself and your work as a witch. I pray you choose the path that leads to a deeper kindness in your relationship with yourself, your community, and your life. Be honest, remember well, and do well with what you remember, Dear Witch. May you be blessed along your path. So it is.

Glossary

altar: *A dedicated space that physically represents your relationship with magic and embodies your metaphysical intentions and on which you enact your rituals*

ancestors: *Consciousness of discarnate and deceased beings that help you connect to the innate magic of your cultural, social, and familial lineages*

banishment: *The act of casting out unwanted energies and beings, with the explicit intent for them to never return*

bundles: *A collection of organic matter meant to embody the energy of a specific intention, season, environment, astrological alignment, etc., and bound together either by wrapping tightly with string or by wrapping up in fabric and tying tightly like a package*

charm: *A magical means of influencing the outcome of a situation by use of a spelled object or chanting a particular phrase as a spoken or sung spell*

correspondence: *A unique resonance between an object, element, or color and an emotion or deep spiritual meaning*

cosmology: *A system of beliefs that help you make sense of your experiences in life and take action on your values*

coven: *A group of witches, or magically minded individuals, who gather regularly to practice their craft and perform rituals; can be public or private, each with their own community guidelines*

divination: *The use of tools and techniques to derive insight and information through supernatural or metaphysical means*

effigies: *An embodied representation of a specific person or entity meant to be used to conjure the attributes of their likeness into a space; often made as sacrificial objects out of organic matter such as wax or plant material*

fixing: *A term rooted in Hoodoo and Conjure and used in American folk magic to describe the anointing and dressing of spell objects with oils, herbs, or the ashes of burnt prayers to affect an outcome*

herbalism: *The intentional study of the therapeutic properties and medicinal application of herbs and plants*

hex/curse: *The casting of a spell or ritual directed toward a person, place, or object and intended to inflict harm, punishment, retribution, or obstruction*

instinct: *An innate or learned response to circumstances and energies; usually emotionally charged; not to be mistaken for intuition*

intuition: *A sense of knowing derived from an innate connection to Source; ability to access information about a situation without cognition*

invocation: *The summoning of supernatural energies or sentient beings for assistance with a particular intention or outcome*

poppets: *An embodied representation of oneself or another living person meant to embody certain attributes of their likeness; often meant to serve as a surrogate and used to transfer energy from the poppet to the person it represents*

prayer: *An intentional conversation with spiritual forces, ancestors, your higher self, or whatever guided energies you're in a relationship with*

ritual: *A series of intentional and repetitive actions meant to connect the soul to greater influences, often performed at specific times of the day, month, year, seasons, or stages of life*

sigil: *A combination of distinct shapes, symbols, words, or other icons meant to embody the symbolic representation of a particular intent, context, and means of a desired outcome*

sovereignty: *The energetic state of self-governance, sacred autonomy, and personal power free from outside influences*

spells: *Ritualized intent meant to harness energy to affect a particular circumstance*

symbol: *A character or object that represents a particular function or concept; used to focus intention*

Wicca: *A pagan religion that draws upon pre-Christian, Western European beliefs and folk practices, popularized by Gerald Brosseau Gardner; Wiccan faith centers on the belief in a supreme Goddess and God, the inherent magic of nature, and the ritualization of life stages and seasonal cycles*

witch's gaze: *The ability of a witch, learned and innate, to direct energy, influence states of being, and access awareness by using their physical and psychic senses to peer into another person or situation*

SCHOOLS

**Black Witch University and Podcast
(Facebook.com/BlackWitchUniversity)**
*A school of magic and media resources for witches of the Black diaspora
to reclaim and reappropriate their magical practices and sacred spaces.*

The Living Altar (livingaltar.com)
This is my ritual art collaboration with Kiki Robinson of The Opulent
Witch; *you can purchase* The Living Altar Oracle Deck *here.*

School of Traditional Magic (traditionalmagic.com)
*The website for my private practice and School of Traditional Magic,
where I offer mentorship, teachings, custom ritual and spell work, and
one-on-one healing sessions.*

The Witches Temple (witchestemple.org)
*This is my home temple where I serve as High Priestess. I founded this
temple as a safer space for underrepresented and marginalized witches
to connect, learn, and grow. We offer in-person and online resources for
classes, healing services, readings, and gatherings.*

BOOKS

**Balkan Traditional Witchcraft by Radomir Ristic
(translated by Michael C. Carter)**
*A modern primer on Balkan traditional witchcraft, centering on
Serbo-Croatian magical practices.*

Emergent Strategy: Shaping Change, Changing Worlds by adrienne maree brown
*A new cosmological framework rooted in social justice, interdependent
"self-help," community resourcing, ecological wisdom, mutual aid, and
radical cultural shift.*

Queer Magic: Power beyond Boundaries by Lee Harrington and Tai Fenix Kulystin
An anthology of queer and trans witches speaking to their experience of crafting a more intersectional community of witches outside of the cisgender, heteronormative patriarchy.

Shades of Faith: Minority Voices in Paganism by Crystal Blanton
An anthology of various experiences of marginalized witches as they navigate the White- and Western European–dominated pagan community.

Witchcraft Activism: A Toolkit for Magical Resistance by David Salisbury
A magical grimoire masterfully crafted by queer activist David Salisbury that details the use of witchcraft as magical resistance to systemic oppression.

Witchery: Embrace the Witch Within by Juliet Diaz
A grimoire by third generation witch Juliet Diaz, providing practical foundations for everyday magic.

PODCASTS

Bespoken Bones by Pavini Moray
A queer- and trans-centered podcast exploring the intersections of ancestry, sexuality, magick, science, and trauma healing.

Ghost of a Podcast by Jessica Lanyadoo
Weekly astrological forecasts and practical advice by queer astrologer, animal communicator, and psychic medium Jessica Lanyadoo.

Rise Up Good Witch by Corinna
Focusing on the radical magic of self care and community support, Corinna weaves astrology, tarot, magic, and herbalism into a salve of resilience through conversations with witches, healers, and activists.

Which Witch Are You? by **Imani Sims and Maisha Manson**
A magic and tarot lifestyle podcast by two queer witches of color centering on their love of food, art, and culture.

TAROT DECKS

Dust II Onyx: A Melanated Tarot by **Courtney Alexander**
A multimedia tarot deck centered around the complex layers of Blackness, featuring cultural myths, symbolism, history, and icons within the Black diaspora.

The Numinous Tarot by **Noel Arthur Heimpel**
A modern tarot deck crafted by agender queer artist Noel Arthur Heimpel. This deck beautifully challenges the lack of marginalized representation common within traditional tarot.

The Slutist Tarot by **Morgan Claire Sirene**
An intersectional, inclusive tarot deck that showcases femme, queer, trans, Black, and indigenous identities and celebrates sex positivity, gender variance, and divine liberation of sensuality.

The Weaver Tarot by **The Threads of Fate**

A queer crafted tarot deck that de-centers the gender binary of the traditional Rider-Waite tarot with bold yet understated imagery.

WEBSITE/WORKSHOPS/ZINES

witchesunionhall.wordpress.com/workshopzine/
A queer witch, anarchist collective offering free and donation-based workshops, zines, and educational materials on topics related to cultural appropriation, queer culture, and witchcraft.

References

Lee, Patrick Jasper. *We Borrow the Earth: An Intimate Portrait of the Gypsy Folk Tradition and Culture.* London: Thorsons, 2000.

Ristic, Radomir. *Balkan Traditional Witchcraft.* Translated by Michael C. Carter. Los Angeles: Pendraig Publishing, 2009.

Robinson, Kiki, and Ylvadroma Marzanna Radziszewski. *The Living Altar: An Oracle and Spell Deck for the Radical Witch.* Seattle: The Living Altar, 2020.

Zakroff, Laura Tempest. *Sigil Witchery: A Witch's Guide to Crafting Magick Symbols.* Woodbury, MN: Llewellyn Publications, 2018.

Index

A

Abundance, 127–129, 148
  anointing oil, 130–131
  values inventory, 135–136
Agnosticism, 26
Air element, 19
Alexandrian Wicca, 7
All-Purpose Blessing Incense, 54–55
All-Purpose Ritual Oil, 56–57
Altars
  about, 26–28
  for community, 98–99
  house, 117
  inner altar meditation, 62–63
Ancestors, 46
Angelica root, 55
Animal companions, 157
Animism, 26
Atheism, 26
Autumn, 20–21
Autumnal equinox, 21–22

B

Balsamic moon, 23
Basil, 55
Bathrooms, 107, 120
Bay leaves, 55
Bedroom Portal, 123–124
Bedrooms, 106
Black (color), 24
Blessings
  all-purpose incense, 54–55
  for animal companions, 157
  bundles, 115–116
  for friends and family, 97
Blue (color), 24
Bundles, 161

C

Candles, 39–40
Carnations, 55
Ceremonial witches, 7–8
Charms, 25
Circles, casting and closing, 29, 31
Cleaning, 108
Colors, 24
Community, 9, 78–79, 98–99
Cord-Cutting Ritual, 85–86
Cords, 43
Correspondences, 14, 40
Covens, 9
Crescent moon, 22
Crystals, 38–39
Cultural appropriation, 46

D

Daily Insight Tarot Spread,
    70–71
Daily life, 151–152
Daily Offerings, 168–169
Daily Protection Ritual, 52–53
Deism, 26
Deities, 25–26
Devil, 3
Difficult choices, 162–163
Disseminating moon, 23
Ditheism, 26
Divination, 25
Doormat Warding, 113–114
Dreams, 160

E

Ease for Traveling, 164–165
Eclectic witches, 6
Effigies, 161

V

Values, 128–129, 135–136
Vernal equinox, 21
Vessels, 41–42
Voice, 43
Void, 19–20

W

Wands, 40
Water element, 19
Wellness Brew, 68–69
Wheel of the Year, 17–18, 28
White (color), 24
Willow leaves, 55

Windfall Spell, 143–144
Window Wards, 111–112
Winter, 20
Winter solstice, 22
Witches and witchcraft
  history of, 2
  misconceptions about, 2–3
  and religion, 4
  types of, 4–8
Witch's Wheel, 17–18, 28

Y

Yarrow, 55
Yellow (color), 24

Acknowledgments

My deepest thanks to my ancestors, my helping spirits, and my amazing community! Thank you to my clients, students, and sibling witches: Your work and dedication to the craft have radicalized and inspired me beyond measure. Thank you to the Black Willow, Hawthorn, Oak, Ivy, Birch, Rowan, Yew, and Apple. Thank you to my daughters and sisters of Hecate. Thank you to all of my witch children; I'm the proudest witch mom!

A special thank you to my dear art partner Kiki Robinson, my creative mentor Colleen Twombly-Borst, and my beloved friends Niko, Keri, Alexis, Sonya, Kook, Melissa, Valeria, Espen, Gil, and Nick for all your guidance and feedback during the process of writing this book.

About the Author

Ylva Mara Radziszewski is a High Priestess, temple tender, traditional witch, teacher, writer, artist, and licensed acupuncturist and herbalist, currently residing on unceded Duwamish (Dkhw'Duw'Absh) and Coast Salish territory, where this book was written. They are known for approaching their work with a commitment to further understanding how access to wellness and traditions of magic are complicated by, and interconnected with, the violence of kyriarchal oppression. Their practice prioritizes the support of sex workers; black, brown, and Indigenous community members; femmes; survivors of trauma and abuse; survivors of incest and assault; chronically ill folx; trans and non-binary specific health concerns; addiction recovery; reproductive health support; folx navigating intergenerational and diasporic trauma; and those seeking alternative and supplemental support for acute chronic mental health concerns. They are the founder of the School of Traditional Magic; co-founder of the radical witch's collective The Witches Temple, formerly The Cunning Crow Apothecary; and co-creatrix of The Living Altar, a ritual and performance art project. For more information:

The School of Traditional Magic
- *Instagram@schooloftraditionalmagic*
- *traditionalmagic.com*

The Living Altar
- Instagram@thelivingaltar
- livingaltar.com

The Witches Temple
- Instagram@communitywitchcraft
- witchestemple.org

CPSIA information can be obtained
at www.ICGtesting.com
Printed in the USA
JSHW011448160720
6738JS00002B/15